A Dissertation Concerning the Angel Who is Called the Redeemer

Peter Allix (1641-1717)

Edited and Compiled
by Douglas Van Dorn

A Dissertation Concerning the Angel Who is Called the Redeemer

Peter Allix (1641-1717)

Edited and Compiled
by Douglas Van Dorn

Waters of Creation Publishing
Dacono, Colorado

This stand-alone Waters of Creation edition: © 2019.

First Published in 1689 as an appendix in *The Judgment of the Ancient Jewish Church, Against the Unitarians*. 1699 edition published by R. Chiswell, London.

This edition of *A Dissertation on the Angel* has been modernized in style and language by the publisher and is copyright.

Cover Design: Doug, Breanna, and Alesha Van Dorn

ISBN- 978-0-9862376-5-2 (Waters of Creation Publishing)

Contents

EDITOR'S INTRODUCTION 1

A DISSERTATION CONCERNING THE ANGEL
WHO IS CALLED THE REDEEMER 13

COMMENTARIES ON GENESIS 48:15-16 51
    JEWISH 51
    CHRISTIAN INTERPRETATIONS 56

EXCERPTS FROM "JUDGMENTS OF THE JEWISH
CHURCH" 77
    CHAP. VIII. 77
    CHAP. XII. 99
    CHAP. XIII. 123
    CHAP. XIV. 139
    CHAP. XV. 159

GLOSSARY OF WORKS AND AUTHORS CITED 183

AUTHOR INDEX 191

SCRIPTURE INDEX 195

Other Books by Waters of Creation

Waters of Creation: A Biblical-Theological Study of Baptism (2009)
Galatians: A Supernatural Justification (2012)
Giants: Sons of the Gods (2013)
Covenant Theology: A Reformed Baptist Primer (2014)
From the Shadows to the Savior: Christ in the Old Testament (2015)
The Unseen Realm: Q & A Companion (2016)
Five Solas (2019)

For more information, articles, radio shows, and broadcasts go to: dougvandorn.com

Editor's Introduction

Reason for This Series

I am convinced, after studying the topic of Christ in the Old Testament in some depth for the last several years, and having lived in modern conservative Reformed and Evangelical Christian circles for nearly 50 years, that too many Christians (past and present) far too often presuppose and/or superimpose a kind of Unitarian grid upon the OT. This is a very Liberal way of reading the Scripture, out of line with orthodox Christian teaching throughout history.

It isn't that this is done malevolently, for these same Christians often do see Christ in the OT in one way or another. I am not talking about a Christianity that outright denies the deity of Jesus. In fact, I'm talking about a Christianity that loves him as the *Theanthropos*—The God-man. It isn't that this is done deliberately either. At least, not usually. I would say it is more of a subconscious decision. We speak about Christ being there in type and shadow, but to say that he was actually there—*in person?* This is a hard pill for many to swallow. I had more than one professor in my conservative Baptist schooling tell the students that to see Christ or a Trinity actually there, as if any of the human authors could have deliberately written about these things when they wrote the OT books, was reading the NT back into the Old. It was eisegesis, not exegesis.

In this way, too many of us presuppose that the Jewish church did not, indeed *could not* have known the Christ in order to write about him actually being present in their midst. He simply wasn't there among them. At best, only the Father was. Yet, somehow, we think, they could foresee his coming. But this is a strange oxymoron, because that would seem to itself presuppose that they knew he already existed, if the Messiah they prophesied about was truly God. But if they knew he already existed, why couldn't he have known them or made himself known to them? Nevertheless, at the end of the day when we ask questions like *Job knew his Redeemer* (Job 19:25) *to be Christ?* Or *Solomon comprehended the Son of a Father who has ascended to heaven* (Prov 30:4) *was Christ?* Or *Abraham believed God* (Gen 15:6), *whom he knew to be Christ?* Not possible is a very common answer to hear.

As a case in point, there is an ancient manuscript variant in Jude 5 where one family of texts say "Jesus" lead Israel in the Exodus, while another family reads the "Lord" did it. Apparently, this discussion has been around for a long, long time. Some scribe was asking the same question: *Jude could call the Savior of the Exodus "Jesus?"* Not possible. So, he changed "Jesus" to "Lord." The renowned NT scholar Bruce Metzger ran into the same skepticism I have run into in conservative circles on this very same variant when he was working on his *Textual Commentary on the Greek New Testament* in a committee with a bunch of other scholars. He wrote, "A majority of the Committee was of the opinion that the [Jesus] reading was difficult to the point of impossibility."[1]

Why? Because we presuppose it, that's why. Therefore, any OT text you can think of where a Christian has argued that we see the Trinity or Christ ("Holy, Holy, Holy" or "Let us make man in our image") must be dismissed out of hand.

The Place of this Work in This Series

The work before you is a volume in the series: Christ in All Scripture, by Waters of Creation Publishing. At present, this series consists or will consist of the following volumes:

---

[1] Bruce Manning Metzger, United Bible Societies, *A Textual Commentary on the Greek New Testament, Second Edition a Companion Volume to the United Bible Societies' Greek New Testament (4th Rev. Ed.)* (London; New York: United Bible Societies, 1994), 657.

4 A Dissertation Concerning the Angel of the LORD

- *A Dissertation Concerning the Angel Who is called the Redeemer and Other Select Passages* by Peter Allix
- *Appearances of the Son of God Under the Old Testament* by John Owen
- *The Worship of the Lord Jesus Christ in the Old Testament* by Gerard De Gols
- *The Angel of the LORD In Early Jewish, Christian, and Reformation History,* a compilation of Allix, Owen, and De Gols
- *Promised, Patterned, and Present: Christ in the Old Testament* by Douglas Van Dorn
- *Jesus: Who, What, Where, When, Why?* by Douglas Van Dorn

It serves as either a supplement or stand-alone book. As a supplement, it belongs with the forthcoming book by Matt Foreman and Douglas Van Dorn on the Angel of the LORD. Matt and I were simply not able to put all the material in that volume that we wanted, and Peter Allix's work fills a needed gap.

This book begins with *A Dissertation Concerning the Angel who is called the Redeemer*. The *Dissertation* is like a letter. Hywel Clifford calls the work, "A brief conversation about [the Angel's] meaning that he had recently had with an unconvinced listener (addressed as 'Sir', and not only with politesse but also with rigour and detail throughout)."[2] Its contents are a deep historical study of Genesis 48:15-16.

---

[2] Hywel Clifford, "The 'Ancient Jewish Church': the anti-Unitarian exegetical polemics of Peter Allix," in *From Zwingli to Amyraut:*

This short passage is a two-verse prayer by Jacob addressed to his son Joseph. It is a crucial text to any study of the Angel of the LORD, but it is often overlooked in modern discussions concerning the identity of this mysterious figure. It reads:

> 15 And he blessed Joseph and said, "The God before whom my fathers Abraham and Isaac walked, the God who has been my shepherd all my life long to this day,
> 16 the Angel who has redeemed me from all evil, bless the boys; and in them let my name be carried on, and the name of my fathers Abraham and Isaac; and let them grow into a multitude in the midst of the earth…"

The key to seeing its importance and how the passage answers the question of the Angel's identity is the poetic parallel:

> The God…
> The God…
> The Angel…

As Allix demonstrates beyond a shadow of a doubt, not only does the grammar necessitate that "the Angel" and "the God" be the same Person, this has also been the view of most of the ancient Church Fathers and,

---

Exploring the Growth of European Reformed Traditions, ed. Jon Balserak and Jim West (Göttingen: V&R Academic, 2017).

more curiously to those who do not know the history, the early Jews. This *Dissertation* is clearly one of the most extensive treatments of the Angel of the LORD as the Divine Christ up to this point in history.

Following the *Dissertation* is a series of quotations by the Church Fathers and the Protestant Reformers. Each quotation has Genesis 48:15-16 in it, though some have content that moves beyond this passage. (For more on what the Fathers and Reformers thought about the Angel, see our book on the Angel and/or consult the quotations in the Owen volume in this series). These quotations act as their own kind of supplement to Allix' work on the passage.

In the larger book in which the *Dissertation* is found (*The Judgment of the Ancient Jewish Church Against The Unitarians in the Controversy Upon the Holy Trinity and the Divinity of Our Blessed Savior*), Allix has several chapters dedicated to thinking about the Angel of the LORD from an early Jewish perspective. He uses these chapters to help convince his reader that the early Jews were not all Unitarians. Far from it. As we should expect, if some Jews before Christ worshiped the One True God, they could not be. These chapters add a more robust Old Testament picture of the Angel than is found in the *Dissertation* alone. Thus, I have transcribed several of them for the sake of helping the reader understand more of the history that lies behind the ancient understanding of this mysterious Angel who is to be found throughout the Old Testament. When the totality of his work is read together, Allix can clearly be seen to be a man writing with a depth of scholarship on this topic that has only in the last few decades begun to be duplicated.

In this light, I would recommend Allix' work for anyone skeptical of the contemporary thesis, and now consensus, of modern scholarship that many Jews of the 1st century and before had some conception of a plurality of Persons in the Godhead. This thesis was first brought to light in modern times in 1977 by the late Dr. Alan Segal, a Jewish professor of religion and Judaic studies at several universities, including Princeton. Segal was no fan of what these Rabbi's themselves dubbed "two powers in heaven." But his book of the same title was the first serious modern study to appear on the vital early Rabbinical view that not all strands of ancient Judaism were Unitarian, though neither were they polytheistic. Scholarship that has pursued this has labeled it as "Binatarian," a monotheistic precursor of Christianity but without a full blown systematic Trinitarianism.[3]

---

[3] A bibliography of relevant works in this field is as follows: Margaret Barker, *The Great Angel: A Study of Israel's Second God* (Louisville, KY: Westminster / John Knox Publishers, 1992); Richard Bauckham "The Throne of God and the Worship of Jesus," in *The Jewish Roots of Christological Monotheism: Papers from the St. Andrews Conference on the Historical Origins of the Worship of Jesus*, ed. C. Newman, J. Davila, and G. Lewis (Leiden: E. J. Brill, 1999): 43-69; Bauckham, *God Crucified: Monotheism & Christology in the New Testament* (Grand Rapids, MI: Eerdmans, 1998); Daniel Boyarin, "The Gospel of the Memra: Jewish

Segal, however, shows no familiarity with Allix or his work on the Angel, nor do several of the other

---

Binitarianism and the Prologue to John," *Harvard Theological Review* 94:3 (July 2001): 243-284; Boyarin, "Two Powers in Heaven; or, The Making of a Heresy," in *The Idea of Biblical Interpretation: Essays in Honor of James L. Kugel* (Leiden: Brill, 2003): 331-370; Jarl E. Fossum *The Image of the Invisible God: Essays on the Influence of Jewish Mysticism on Early Christology* (Göttingen: Vandenhoeck and Ruprecht, 1995); Fossum, *The Name of God and the Angel of the LORD: Samaritan and Jewish Concepts of Intermediation and the Origin of Gnosticism* (Tubingen: J. C. B. Mohr, 1985); Simon Gathercole, *The Pre-Existent Son: Recovering the Christologies of Matthew, Mark, and Luke* (Grand Rapids: Eerdmans, 2006); Darrell D. Hannah, *Michael and Christ: Michael Traditions and Angel Christology in Early Christianity*, Wissenschaftliche Untersuchungen zum Neuen Testament 109 (Tübingen: Mohr-Siebeck, 1999); Michael S. Heiser, "The Divine Council in Late Canonical and Non-Canonical Second Temple Jewish Literature." A Dissertation at the University of Wisconsin-Madison (2004); Heiser, *The Unseen Realm: Rediscovering the Supernatural Worldview of the Bible* (Bellingham, WA: Lexham Press, 2015); Larry W. Hurtado, "What Do We Mean by 'First-Century Jewish Monotheism'?" in *Society of Biblical Literature 1993 Seminar Papers*, ed. E. H. Lovering Jr. (Atlanta: Scholars Press, 1993): 348-368; Hurtado, *One God, One Lord: Early Christian Devotion and Ancient Jewish Monotheism* (Philadelphia: Fortress, 1988); Hurtado, *Lord Jesus Christ: Devotion to Jesus in Earliest Christianity* (Grand Rapids: Eerdmans, 2003); Hurtado, "First-Century Jewish Monotheism," *Journal for the Study of the New Testament* 71 (1998): 3-26; Hurtado, "The Binitarian Shape of Early Christian Worship," in *The Jewish Roots of Christological Monotheism, Papers from the St. Andrews Conference on the Historical Origins of the Worship of Jesus*, ed. by Carey C. Newman, James R. Davila and Gladys S. Lewis, Supplements to the Journal for the Study of Judaism, ed. John J. Collins (Leiden: E. J. Brill, 1999): 187-213; Hurtado, *How on Earth Did Jesus Become a God?: Historical Questions about Earliest Devotion to Jesus* (Grand Rapids: Eerdmans, 2005); Aquila H. I. Lee, *From Messiah to Pre-existent Son*, Wissenschaftliche Untersuchungen zum Neuen Testament 192 (Tübingen: Mohr-Siebeck, 2005; reprinted Wipf and Stock, 2009); Alan F. Segal, *Two Powers in Heaven: Early Rabbinic Reports about Christianity and Gnosticism* (Leiden: E. J. Brill, 1977); Loren T. Stuckenbruck and Wendy E. S. North, eds., *Early Jewish and Christian Monotheism*, Journal for the Study of the New Testament, Supplement Series 263, Early Christianity in Context Series (New York: T&T Clark International, 2004).

prominent names in the field.[4] This alone makes republication indispensable. Given the newness of this field of study in modern times, Allix was surely centuries ahead of his time. The title of his work is to prove this very point made so persuasively by Segal and those who have followed him. He is even familiar with the concept of "two powers," though I have not transcribed this portion of his book here (they are in chs. 8–9 in his book), as it wasn't as germane to my purposes as were other parts. I do, however, take it up in my *Promised, Patterned, and Present: Christ in the Old Testament* book in this same series.

    I should point out that it isn't that even Allix was the first to see these things, as he himself goes to great lengths to point out. Even a few decades earlier, John Owen had shown signs of the same stream of influence (see my book by Owen in this series).

    But unlike Owen, it is the depth of this study that truly staggers. Allix' *Dissertation* is brilliantly argued and overwhelming in its citations of ancient material in support of the view that the Angel of the LORD is the Second Person of the Trinity. It covers an astonishing breadth of writers, both contemporary to Allix and ancient. These include ancient and medieval Jews, Church Fathers, medieval Roman Catholics,

---

[4] These include Michael Heiser, Larry Hurtado, Margaret Barker, Richard Bauckham, Daniel Boyarin, Jarl Fossum, Simon Gathercole, and others. There are a few exceptions such as Loren Stuckenbruck, but this is a minority.

Reformers, and other commentators contemporary to his time. His familiarity of the history is masterful. His knowledge of the issues is astonishing. Indeed, it is difficult to fathom how anyone could even gain access to so many obscure works, let alone read them all in their original languages (Hebrew, Greek, Latin, Spanish, French, and English), and then cull the relevant material into a single decisive book. Therefore, I present Peter Allix on the Angel of the LORD so that the modern reader might become acquainted with this brilliant Christ-centered conservative Reformed theologian so long out of print.

Peter Allix

Who was Peter Allix? As the *Dictionary of National Biography* tells it, Peter (Pierre) Allix was born in 1641, the son of Pierre Allix, pastor of the Reformed Church of France at Alençon, where he was born. He attended protestant universities in Saumur and Sedan. He was distinguished in Hebrew and Syriac and used it to work on a new translation of the Bible. He became a pastor at St. Agobille in Champagne, France, but was soon moved in 1670 to Paris to preside over the principle Reformed church of the city. By 1685, due to political unrest, he fled France for England, where he quickly learned the language, nationalized, and began publishing. He received a D. D. from Oxford and Cambridge in 1690. His popularity and reputation as a preeminent preacher and scholar soon reached none other than Louis XIV, who wanted him to return to France. Allix staunchly refused. He died in 1717.

A Note on Editing

I have updated typos and mistakes in citations, as well as antiquated terms and phrases from Allix's 1821 Clarendon Press edition (though I also had to consult the 1699 edition). I have transliterated all Greek and Hebrew and translated some of the foreign languages that were left alone previously. In many cases I have used the ESV for the biblical citation, though any time I felt the original (often the KJV or Geneva Bible) made the point more strongly, I have retained it or made my own translation as close to the original, but with modern language.

Whenever I could track down a modern English translation of a work in a footnote, I have changed the older citations to fit the modern. In other cases, I have left the citation and its reference unchanged. It is up to the reader to track those down. Most of the Scripture passages quoted were originally italicized. I have retained this and italicized the Targum quotations as well. Capitalization was a bit of a subjective decision. Old English capitalized many more words than we do. If I feel a word in any way applied to an attribute or name of God, it remains capitalized.

My hope is that being confronted by Allix, and the myriads of Jews, Church Fathers, and Reformers that he discusses will help settle the reader into a sure and certain confidence as to the much questioned fact that the OT Church did in fact know and worship the Lord Jesus Christ, especially when he came to them as the Angel of the LORD, who is, in fact, the Second Person of the Holy Trinity, the Son pre-incarnate, the Redeemer whom those people before Messiah came knew, trusted in, and worshiped as Yahweh-God.

A more important topic is difficult to discern, especially in days like ours when the OT has fallen on such hard times. Reading others who have gone before us talk about Christ in the OT in such clear, profound, and direct ways should be a balm to the soul of any Christian and a powerful apologetic against unbelief.

Doug Van Dorn
November 2019

A Dissertation Concerning the Angel Who is called the Redeemer

SIR,

YOU DO VERY TRULY observe, that the subject of our last but short conversation is a matter of the greatest moment and deserving the utmost care in the discussion of it. When mention was made there of the Angel, whose blessing Jacob prayed might descend on the sons of Joseph, I asserted he was none other than the *Logos*, or Word. You were not then very inclined to embrace this notion, being carried away with the authority of some great names, especially of Grotius,[5] who understands this Angel in Jacob's prayer to be only a created angel.

But having not the time to hear the grounds of my assertion, you were desirous I should put them with whatever clarity I could into writing, in hopes that the same arguments, if they should prove cogent to bring you over to my opinion, might be of use to others who were in the same sentiments with yourself. So with this good end being proposed, I set myself without delay to your commands; and having digested my thoughts in this paper, I now send them to you, entreating you to judge of them, as you are inclined of the labors of your friend, with all impartiality and humanity, still remembering that I made it my only care to express my thoughts clearly, and to find out the truth, and to deliver it naturally, according to the best of my understanding. And so, I come to the question in hand.

SECT. I.

MOSES HAVING RELATED how Joseph took his two sons along with him to Jacob his father that lay sick, in order to obtain his blessing on them before he died,

---

[5] Hugo Grotius (1583-1645). Dutch Jurist and Arminian theologian, he is noted for his "governmental" or "moral government" theory of the atonement and for being imprisoned for his views.

goes on to give us the form in which he blessed them, Gen 48:15-16:

> ¹⁵ And he blessed Joseph and said, "The God before whom my fathers Abraham and Isaac walked, the God who has been my shepherd all my life long to this day,
> ¹⁶ the angel who has redeemed me from all evil, bless the boys; and in them let my name be carried on, and the name of my fathers Abraham and Isaac; and let them grow into a multitude in the midst of the earth."

These words are thus rendered by the Greek Interpreters, commonly called the Septuagint:

> ¹⁵ And he blessed them and said, "The God, whom my fathers Abraham and Isaac were pleasing before him, the Lord who nourishes me from youth to day, this
> ¹⁶ the angel who rescues me from all evils, may he bless these children, and in them my name and the name of my fathers Abraham and Isaac will be invoked, and may they be multiplied into a great multitude upon the earth.[6]

And in the Latin version;

---

[6] Rick Brannan et al., eds., *The Lexham English Septuagint* (Bellingham, WA: Lexham Press, 2012), Ge 48:15–16.

> ¹⁵ And Jacob blessed the sons of Joseph, and said: God, in whose sight my fathers Abraham and Isaac walked, God that feeds me from my youth until this day:
> ¹⁶ The angel that delivers me from all evils, bless these boys: and let my name be called upon them, and the names of my fathers Abraham and Isaac; and may they grow into a multitude upon the earth.[7]

You see there is little or no difference between these versions and the Hebrew, with which also agrees the Spanish version of Athias and Usquez, which was printed in the last age at Ferrara,[8] and which is of great authority with the Jews and serves in the place of the Hebrew text to those who cannot read it. It renders indeed, *The God who fed me*, by *El dio governan a mi*, and the word *goel who has redeemed me*, by *El redimien a mi*, or, *my Redeemer*; but the sense is not altered at all.

Drusius[9] notes in his fragments of the ancient interpreters of the Old Testament that the participle *goel* here attributed to the Angel, is rendered *agchisteus* by

---

[7] *The Holy Bible, Translated from the Latin Vulgate* (Bellingham, WA: Logos Bible Software, 2009), Ge 48:15–16. Language slightly modernized.

[8] Allix refers here to The Ferrara Bible of 1553, which was paid for and made by Yom-Tov Ben Levi Athias (the typographer) and Abraham ben Salomon Usque the translator) and dedicated to the Duke of Ferrara. It was a translation of an older circulating Spanish translation.

[9] Johannes van den Driesche (1550-1616). Flemish Protestant divine who was an Orientalist, Christian Hebraist, and exegete.

the Greek translators in Ruth 4:8, which imports the next of kin to whom the right of inheritance belongs and with it the relict of his deceased relation. From this translation of the word, St. Jerome, and after him many other divines, taking this Angel to be the Messiah, have collected a relation peculiar of this Angel to the family of Jacob, of which the Messiah was to be born.[10] Christ, he says, shall come and redeem us with his blood; who, as the Hebrew has it, is of kin to Zion, and is descended from the stock of Israel; for so the word *goel* or *agchisteus* signifies.

But there is another sense of the words, *g'l* and *goel* and according to which the Greek interpreters do more commonly render them, I mean that of *lutroun* and *lutrōtēs*, which confirms the use of the like word in the Spanish version. If you would see the places, you may consult Kircher's Concordance.[11]

The whole difficulty therefore of the place may be reduced to three heads, which I shall propose by way of question:

I. Whether the *elohim* spoken of in vs. 15 is the very YHWH [or YHVH or Yahweh or LORD] whom the Jews acknowledge for their God?

---

[10] Jerome on Isaiah 59.
[11] Nearly 300 years before Strong would publish his famous concordance (in 1890), the Lutheran Conrad Kircher published a concordance of the Greek Septuagint in 1607.

II. Whether the mentioned in vs. 16 is the same as the *elohim* in vs. 15 or differs from him as a creature does from its Creator?

III. Whether the prayer contained in Jacob's blessing is made to God alone, or to the redeeming Angel together with him?

SECT. II.

IN ANSWER TO THE FIRST QUESTION we do not need to look far: for Onkelos[12] in his Chaldee [i.e. Aramaic] paraphrase expounds the word *elohim* by *YHVH*. Jonathan has done the same in his version. Nor do I know any Christian who ever blamed them for it. Why should they? Since it is evident for those who consider this text carefully, as the Christians generally do the holy Scriptures, that these Targumists have faithfully expressed the mind of Jacob.

Jacob had been remembering that appearance where God had blessed him at Luz, in these words,

---

[12] This is the Aramaic Targum Onkelos. A Targum is a paraphrastic rendition of the Hebrew Scripture into Aramaic for Jews who did not speak Hebrew. They were probably written down around the first century by Jews. Genesis has three main Targums: Onkelos, Neofiti, and Pseudo-Jonathan (which he cites next). To help with their differences, think of them like the *NIV*, *The Living Bible*, and *The Message*, in that order. They can be mostly literal like Onkelos, or more adventuresome like Pseudo-Jonathan.

"God Almighty appeared to me at Luz in the land of Canaan, and blessed me, and said to me, 'Behold, I will make you fruitful, and multiply you, and I will make of you a multitude of people; and give this land to your descendants [seed] *after you as an everlasting possession'"* (Gen 48:3-4).[13] Now what can be more absurd than to imagine that Jacob, when he blesses Joseph's sons and prays for the increase of his posterity by them, would direct his prayers to anyone other than the one whose kindnesses he had so abundantly experienced, and whose promises for the multiplication of his seed were even now fresh in his memory?

This I thought fit to observe against those of the Jews that doubt of it, following as they think the author of the book of Genesis Rabbah[14] who notes that a lesser title is given to the Angel than to him who is called *Elohim*; as if he had a mind thereby to tell us that by the angel here mentioned, Jacob meant a mere angel and not God.

If the author of Genesis Rabbah had understood this of a created angel, he certainly made a very great mistake. For, besides the absurdity of this opinion, it is a blasphemy to suppose that Abraham and Isaac are

---

[13] The 1821 edition does not quite read like the KJV, but it is close. So, I have used the NKJV for better readability here and in many places.
[14] Written between 300-500 A.D., *Genesis Rabbah* is a midrash (interpretation) of ancient rabbinical sermons interpreting the book of Genesis. The reference in the margin is *Mattenot Kehun* [*Matnoth Kehunah*], f. 23. Col. 4. And f. 108. Col. 3.

commended for walking before the angel as Jacob asserts they did before God. "*God,*" he says, "*before whom my fathers Abraham and Isaac walked*" (Gen 48:15). For the word "to walk" in this place comprehends all the acts of their religion throughout their whole lives, and so Moses uses the word to describe the entire obedience of Enoch (Gen 5:22). A modern Jew, R. Salomon Aben Melek,[15] acknowledges in his *The Perfection of Beauty* on this place, that the word *to walk* denotes the worship of the heart which a creature owes to God.

But that the author of the Rabbah understood it of an uncreated Angel, who is often called in the Old Testament *Elohim* and *Jehovah* and *Jehovah Elohim*, I little doubt, because he quotes the same authority in this place, which we meet with in *Bab. Talm. Pesachim*[16] (cap. x. fol. 118. col. 1). And which makes this Angel to be God.[17]

---

[15] The "R." refers to Rabbi. Solomon ben Melek was from Fez, in modern Morocco. Little is known of him. He published his Bible commentary *Michlol Jophi* (*Perfection of Beauty*) in 1549 through a press in Constantinople. It was later published in 1660 and 1685 in Amsterdam by Jacob Abendana.

[16] The Talmud is the long, written oral traditions of the Jews written down in the centuries after the destruction of the temple in 70 A.D. "Pesachim," in the Babylonian Talmud, is mostly taken up with the laws of Passover and the lamb offering.

[17] The Talmud can be difficult to figure out what is original and what is not. This reference is a good case-study. For instance, in Neusner's English edition, the Hebrew reads that R. Yohanan said, "Providing food for a person is more difficult than redemption, for with respect to redemption, it is written, 'The angel who has redeemed me from all evil' (Gen. 48:16) … of food: 'the God who has fed me' (Gen. 48:15)." This seems to support Allix' point. But when you add the Aramaic you get, "Providing food for a person is more

But if he was of another mind, we might have other Jews, and of no less authority, to oppose to him. These understand it as we do. Particularly, we have the prayers of the Jewish Church. Many of them allude to this and places like it in Genesis as saying they refer only to God exclusively, and not from a created angel, for he has the title of Redeemer, who delivers from all evil (see *Talm. Hier. tr. Berac.* cap. 4. fol. 8. col. 1. and their Liturgies).

I know Cyril of Alexandria[18] would have Jacob to understand God the Father by *Elohim* (vs. 15), and the eternal Son of God by the redeeming Angel. He confirms this explication with Ephesians 1:2, "*Grace be to*

---

difficult than redemption, for with respect to redemption, it is written, 'The angel who has redeemed me from all evil' (Gen. 48:16) *thus an everyday angel was enough*; of food: 'the God who has fed me' (Gen. 48:15)." (Jacob Neusner, *The Babylonian Talmud: A Translation and Commentary*, vol. 4 [Peabody, MA: Hendrickson Publishers, 2011], 546). This obviously makes his point null and void. But, again, it is not in the original Hebrew and it is clear that Allix is not reading any edition that merges both languages into a single text.

Another edition reads very much like the Aramaic addition. "R. Johanan said again: The earning of a man's daily bread is beset with more difficulty than the redemption; for concerning the redemption it is written [Gen. 48:16]: 'The angel who redeemed me from all evil,' while concerning a man's daily bread it is written [ibid. 15]: 'The God who fed me from my first being unto this day,' whence we see that for redemption it only required an angel, while for the sustenance of a man it required God's providence." (Michael L. Rodkinson, tran., *The Babylonian Talmud: Original Text, Edited, Corrected, Formulated, and Translated into English*, vol. 5 (Boston, MA: The Talmud Society, 1918), 250–251). Curiously, many online editions do not have this section at all!

[18] Lib. vi. in Gen. p. 210. This is found in Cyril's *Glaphyrorum in Genesim* (*Elegant Comments on Genesis*) in *Patrologia Graeca* (PG), vol. 69.

you, and peace from God our Father, and the Lord Jesus Christ," because grace is nothing but the blessing of God communicated to the Church by the Father and the Son. But St. Chrysostom's[19] opinion is much more probable to me, who asserts *Elohim* to be the eternal Son of God, that is described in both the fifteenth and sixteenth verses by different titles.

In this he followed all the ancient Christians, who used to ascribe to the Son all the appearances of God or of the Angel of Jehovah that are mentioned by Moses; and who teach in particular, that the blessing of the *Logos* was prayed for by Jacob in this place.

I have no misgivings in asserting that the ancient Christians ascribed all the appearances of God in Moses' writings to the eternal *Logos*, having the following authorities for my assertion. Justin Martyr, *Against Trypho*; Clement of Alexandria, *The Instructor* 1.7; Tertullian, *Against the Jews* 9; Origen, *On Isaiah* 6; Cyprian, *Against the Jews* 2.5; *Apostolic Constitutions* 5.20; Eusebius, *Church History* 1.3; Cyril, *Catechetical Lectures* 12.16; *The Council of Sirmium* (351), Canon 13;[20]

---

[19] Homily 66. In Gen. p. 7.
[20] The original reference appears to be slightly off. Variously numbered 15 or 14, the first reads, "If anyone says that the Son did not appear to Abraham, but the unbegotten God, or a part of Him, let him be anathema." The next reads, "If anyone says that the Son did not wrestle with Jacob as a man, but the unbegotten God, or a part of Him, let him be anathema." The next, "If anyone understands the words, 'Then the Lord rained fire from the Lord' (Gen 19:24), not as referring to the Father and the Son, but says that He (the Father) sent rain from Himself, let him be anathema. For the Lord the Son sent rain from the Lord the Father. See Charles Joseph

Gregory of Elvira, *On Faith*; Theodoret of Cyrus, *Questions on Exodus* 5; Leo, *Letter 31 to Pulcheria*, and many others. In like manner, they refer to the Word, those appearances of God, which he promised to Abraham, Isaac, and Jacob himself, as you may see in Justin Martyr, *Apology*, for those to Abraham and Isaac; and for those to Jacob, in Clement of Alexandria, *The Instructor* 1.7; Novatian, *On the Trinity* 26, 27; Procopius of Gaza in h. 1.

In this, the ancient Christians did no more than the even older Jews did before them, who by *Elohim* in this place did not understand a created angel, but the *Logos*, whom the Targumists and the strictest followers of their fathers' traditions are wont to express by the *Shekinah* (Glory) and the *Memra* (Word).

Philo makes all the appearances which we meet with in the books of Moses to belong to the Word, and the latter Cabalists (since Christ's time) not only do the same, but deny that the Father ever appeared, saying, it was the *Logos* only that manifested himself to their fathers, whose proper name is *Elohim*. For this consult R. Menachem de Rekanati,[21] from *Genesis Rabbah* on the *Parasch* (see *Bresch.* f. 14. c. 3. *Ed. Ven.* and on *Par.* לך לך, f. 30. c. 1).

Hefele, "72. New Synod and First Formula of Sirmium in 351," in *A History of the councils of the Church from the Original Documents*, vol. 2 A.D. 326 to 429, (Edinburgh: T&T Clark, 1896), 196.

[21] Menahem ben Benjamin Recanati (1223-1290). Italian rabbi who wrote a commentary on the Torah.

I have often wondered how it came to pass, that most of the Divines of the Church of Rome, who would seem to have the greatest veneration for antiquity, would so much despise it in this question, while the ancient Jewish and Christian Church agree. Sanctius[22] in his notes on Acts 7 says it is a difficult question among Divines, whether God's appearances in Scripture were performed immediately by God himself, or by his angels. And then having cited several ancient Fathers who thought it was the *Logos* that appeared, he adds, "But currently, the theologians prefer that judgment which states that in the ministry of angels a divine form was presented to ancient people; this is the judgment of Dionysius, etc."[23] Lorinus,[24] another Jesuit, says something similar in Acts 7:31.

But this is not the worst of it, that they forsake the judgment of the ancients; for they also make bold to contradict the plain words of Christ himself in John 1:18. Christ says, "*No man has seen God at any time, the only-begotten who is in the bosom of the Father he has declared him.*" And parallel to this text is John 6:46. Certainly he must be very blind who does not see that Christ in

---

[22] Gaspar Sanchez (1553-1628). Spanish Jesuit. Taught at Oropesa in Madrid. Spent thirteen years writing commentaries on Scripture.
[23] Thanks to Arjen Vreugdenhil for the translation.
[24] Lorinus of Avignon (1559-1634). *The Cambridge Encyclopedia of the Jesuits* has only one entry for "Lorinus." It reads, "Three other Jesuits are known to have published commentaries on Scripture, but beyond their names and the approximate time in which they lived, not much is known of them."

these words not only denies that the Father had showed himself in those appearances that were made to the ancient patriarchs, but that he also ascribes them to himself and not to the angels.

Away then with such Divines who, setting aside the authority of Christ, choose to theologize in the principal heads of religion according to the sense and prejudices of the modern Jews. We do not desire to be wiser in these matters than the primitive Christians were, among whom it passed for an established truth, that the *Elohim* in Jacob's prayer was the very Jehovah of the Jews, termed by them sometimes as *Shekinah*, and sometimes as *Memra*.

SECT. III.

AS TO THE SECOND QUESTION it would be no question at all, but for the obstinacy of some latter Jews. He who reads the Hebrew text without prejudice cannot but see that the Elohim in vs. 15. is called *ha-melek ha-goel 'oti* (*"the angel who has redeemed me"*) in the following verse. Thus, it follows that this redeeming Angel is *Jehovah*.

Because this opinion is contradicted by some of the chief modern Jews such as Abarbanel[25] and Alshek[26] on this place, and by most of the Popish Divines, as well as by a few of the Reformed that have not sifted this matter accurately, we will offer some proofs for the conviction of those who are not obstinately bent against the truth.

1. If Jacob had two Persons in his mind as different as God and a created angel are, he would have coupled them together by the particle which is not only conjunctive, but very proper to distinguish the Persons of whom we speak. He would have said, "*God before whom my Fathers walked, God who fed me from my youth; and the Angel that delivered me, bless the lads.*" But Jacob is so far from doing this that on the contrary he puts a ה (*he*) demonstrative before the "Angel," just as he did before "God," without any copulative between. This sufficiently demonstrates that he means the same Person by God and the Angel. Munsterus[27] was well aware of this, and therefore being willing to distinguish the

---

[25] Don Isaac Abravanel (1437-1508). Jewish statemen, religious Jew, scholar, Bible commentator and philosopher of the "Spanish Golden Age."

[26] Moshe Alshich (1508-1593). Prominent rabbi, preacher, commentator. Little is known of him. Legend says his son was kidnapped as a child and became a Muslim and that a special prayer was written for his return.

[27] Sebastian Münster (1488-1552). German cartographer, cosmographer, and Christian Hebraist scholar. Early on he was a Franciscan, then became Lutheran to accept a chair at the University of Basel.

redeeming Angel from God, he translates it with an addition, the Angel also.

2. It cannot be easily supposed that Jacob would, in a prayer, use the singular verb *ybrk* ("to bless") as saying the same thing of two persons so very different in their natures as are the Creator and a creature. He certainly ought to have said, "God and the angel" (*ybrcu*, the plural form) may they bless the lads, if he had spoken of two. But his speaking in the singular, "may he bless," is an argument of his having in his eye one Person alone, whose blessing he asked for his seed. Otherwise it would have been a prayer of a strange composition; for according to Athanasius, nowhere do we find that one prays to God and the angel, or any other created being at the same time for anything. Nor is there any similar instance of such a form as this, "God and an angel give you this."

3. But setting aside those rules with which the contrary opinion can never be reconciled, consider the thing itself in Jacob's prayer, and you will find it absurd to distinguish between the offices of God and those of a created angel toward Jacob. The office ascribed to God is feeding him from his youth; the office ascribed to the angel is delivering him from all evil; which must be very distinct offices, if the Persons are to be distinguished. And so R. Jochanan[28] accounts them (*Gem.*

---

[28] R. Yohanan ben Zeccai (30-90 A.D.). A primary contributor to the core text of the Mishnah.

Pesasch. fol. 118). Though he believes the Angel to be the same with *Elohim*, yet he contends that feeding, the greater work, is attributed to God; and delivering, the lesser work, to an angel. The same thing is said by the author of Jalkut[29] on this place; and R. Samuel[30] on the book Rabboth above mentioned. But in the phrase of these Jewish masters this distinction is very insipid; it is harshly formed, without considering that Jacob in this blessing reflected on the words of the vow which he made at Luz and afterwards called Bethel, because of God's appearing to him there.

Now, these were the words of Jacob's vow, "*If God will be with me, and keep me in the way in which I shall walk: if he will give meat to eat, and clothing to put on, and bring me home in safety to the house of my father, then shall the Lord be my God*" (Gen 28:20-21). Here you see it is from God that Jacob expects to be kept in his way, *i.e.* to be redeemed from all evils that might happen, and that he esteems this to be no less a benefit than sustenance or clothing, which he mentions in the second place. Here is no angel spoken of; and since the redeeming Angel is to be expounded from this place, he cannot be a created angel, for here is no other spoken of but the Lord.

4. By fancying him a created angel who delivered Jacob from all evil, they make Jacob to be a mere

---

[29] R. Shimeon of Frankfurt (13th cent.). Jalkut is a collection of commentaries from various ancient books.
[30] One of the early rabbinical authorities cited in Genesis Rabbah.

idolater, as ascribing to a creature that which belongs only to the Lord of the creation. The Scripture appropriates to God the title of Redeemer, *kat exochen*; nor do godly men ever say of a creature that it delivers them from all evil. David, I am sure, never does; but when he speaks of *"the tribulations of the righteous"* he adds, *"but the Lord delivers him out of all"* (Ps 34:19). And Jacob on another occasion directs his prayer to the Lord that appeared to him at Luz, saying, *"Save me from the hand of my brother Esau, for I fear him much"* (Gen 32:9, 10, 11).

5. God, as I said, has so appropriated the name of Redeemer to himself, so that Jacob could not without sacrilege communicate this title to any creature, no matter how excellent. We cannot be ignorant that David makes this the proper name of God (Ps 19:14), as does Isa 23:14 and 47:4. And this Jonathan confesses on Isa 63:16 in these words, *"You are our Redeemer, your name is from everlasting,"*[31] *i.e.* this is the name that was designed for God from the beginning; which yet cannot hold true, if in Gen 48:16 Jacob is talking about a created angel.

6. It appears plainly from Genesis 49 that Jacob neither desired nor expected any blessing from a created angel, but only from God. Thus he prays, *"The*

---

[31] "Jonathan" appears to be a reference to the Targum by Jonathan ben Uziel. But while this targum does have these words, so does the Scripture itself. The Targum does reference Abraham here, but not Jacob.

God of your father shall be your helper, and the Almighty shall bless you with the blessings of heaven above..." (Gen 49:25). Not a word of a mere angel that redeemed him from all evil; so far was the Patriarch in his former blessing from begging of an angel the multiplication of his seed, which was the only thing which he could now expect of God, as the Jews own (see *Bechai Prof, in Pent*. fol. 1. c. 1).

7. The same conclusion may be drawn from the very order of Jacob's prayer. Had Jacob intended a created angel by the one he says redeemed him from evil, and whose intercession with God he signifies on behalf of his children, would he not have prayed to the angel in the first place? It was most rational to do so. He who wants the interest of a great man to introduce him to the king does not in the first place direct his petition to the king immediately, but first to the great man, and afterwards by him to the king. Let the Papists therefore look to the absurdity of their proceeding, while they pray first to God, and then to saints and angels. Let those Jews who are of the mind of Isaac Abarbanel and Franco Serrano,[32] in his Spanish notes on this place, and contend for angel-worship, see how they can clear themselves of this difficulty, as well as reconcile

---

[32] Joseph Franco Serrano (1652-1695). Rabbi, teacher of Hebrew at the Portuguese synagogue in Amsterdam. He provided a Spanish translation of the books of Moses with marginal notes from the Talmud and the Rabbis who commented on them.

themselves with those ancienter Jews who abhorred this sort of idolatry (Maimonides, *Per, Misna ad tit. Sank.* c. xi).

SECT. IV.

HOW FIRM THESE REASONS ARE that the angel we are speaking about is uncreated and not a created angel is, I hope, evident to everyone. Something, however, of great importance may be still added to illustrate this weighty argument, and that is the judgment of the ancient synagogue. The most ancient Jewish writers, and those who received the traditional doctrine from them, though mortal enemies of the Christian religion, still agree with the Christians in the sense of this text. For, God be thanked, such truths were not renounced all at once by these enemies of our faith. Rather, they began to conceal or discard them by degrees, as they found those arguments turning against themselves in their disputes with the Christians.

To begin with the writings of the Jews before Christ, we find it is God the Word, ver. 12. who is described as he that delivers from all evil, in the Book of Wisdom (Wis 16:8, 12),[33] no doubt with respect to this

---

[33] "And in this you made your enemies confess, that it is you who delivers from all evil ... For neither herb nor poultice cured them, but it was your Word, O Lord, that helps all people."

place, where he takes the angel that delivered Jacob from all evil, to be God.

The same doctrine can be found in Philo the Jew, who lived both before and during the life of Christ (20 B.C. – 50 A.D.). He expressly affirms of the Angel that delivered Jacob from all evil, that he was the *Logos*.[34] And so does Onkelos in his Chaldee paraphrase, translating the words of Jacob naturally, as they lie in the text, without any addition.

Jonathan[35] indeed seems to be of another mind in his paraphrase which runs thus, "*God before whom my fathers Abraham and Isaac worshipped, the Lord that fed me from the time I began to be till this day, may be pleased that the Angel may bless the lads, whom you have ordained to deliver me from all evil.*" Here he distinguishes the Angel from God; but that he did not mean a creature by this Angel is clear, for in other places he translates this Angel by the Word, or *mmr' dvvy* (or *mymr' dyy*, that is "Word of the Lord, cf. Gen 15:6), and especially in that remarkable place where the same Angel is treated in Isa 63:8-10, he says it was the *Word* who redeemed Israel out of all their afflictions.

---

[34] The margin note has Allegor. Ii. P. 71. D. In *Allegorical Interpretation* III 177 we read, "But these men pray to be nourished by the Word (*Logos*) of God: But Jacob, raising his head above the Word, says that he is nourished by God himself, and his words are as follows ... and he speaks of the angel, which is the word, as the physician of his evils, in this speaking most naturally."

[35] Targum Pseudo-Jonathan.

Let us pass on to the Jews after Christ's time, and show that they did not immediately renounce the doctrine of their forefathers.

The author of the book of Zohar[36] (Par. ויהי Fol. 123) has these words, which he repeats often afterwards, *"Come, see the Angel that redeemed me"* is the Shekinah that went along with him.

This is sufficiently intimated by the ancient author Tanchuma,[37] in his book Jelammedenu,[38] who notes on Exodus 33 that the Jews would not have a created angel to go before them, but God himself, in these words, *"Moses answered, I will not have an angel, but your own self."* Now the Jewish commentators on this place of Exodus 33 explain of the *Shekinah*, the words, *"your own self,"* and always distinguish the *Shekinah* from all created beings.

R. Solomon in his notes on this text has these words, *"The Angel that delivered me,"* i.e. The Angel who was accustomed to be sent to me in my affliction (Gen 31) as it is said, *"And the Angel of God spoke to me in a dream, saying, Jacob, I am the God of Bethel,"* etc.

The note of R. Moses Ben Nachman[39] on Genesis 48:16 is very remarkable. *"'The redeeming Angel,'* he

---

[36] The foundational text of the Kabbalah.
[37] Tanchuma bar Abba. Jewish Rabbi (fl. 350-71).
[38] A popular Homily-Midrash originating in Israel after the 8th century. It bears Tanchuma's name but was not written by him.
[39] Moses ben Nahman (1194-1270). Leading medieval Jewish scholar, rabbi, philosopher, physician, kabbalist, and biblical commentator. He lived most of his life in Girona, Catalonia (Spain).

says, is he who answered him in the time of his affliction, and who said to him, '*I am the God of Bethel,*' etc. '*he,*' of whom it is said, that '*my name* is in him.'" He says the same thing on Exodus 3 where the appearance in the bush is mentioned: "'*This is he of whom it is said, and God called Moses out of the bush.*' He is called an Angel, because he governs the world; for it is written in one place, And '*Jehovah,*' that is, the '*Lord God, brought us out of Egypt;*' and in another place, '*He sent his Angel and brought as out of Egypt.*' And again, '*The Angel of his presence saved them,*' viz. that Angel who is the face of God, of whom it is said, '*My face shall go before you.*' Lastly, that Angel of whom the prophet Malachi mentions, '*And the Lord whom you seek shall suddenly come to his temple, even the Angel of the covenant, whom you desire.*'" At length he adds, "The face of God is God himself, as all interpreters do acknowledge; but none can rightly understand this without being instructed in the mysteries of the Law."

R. Menachem of Rekan on Genesis 48:16, is the same who later commented on the whole Pentateuch, was no stranger to this notion. "He means the Shekinah, says he, when he speaks of the redeeming Angel" (f. 52. See also f. 55).

Similarly, R. Bechai,[40] the famous Jewish writer, whose comments are constantly in the hands of the

---

[40] Bahya ben Asher ibn Halawa (1255-1340). Distinguished Spanish rabbi who wrote a commentary on the Hebrew Bible.

Jewish Doctors. He proves that this blessing is not different from that which is afterwards repeated in Genesis 49 where no angel is mentioned. Thus, it follows that the three terms in Gen 48, "*God ... God that fed me ... the Angel that redeemed me,*" are synonymous to the Mighty One of Jacob (Gen 49:25), the title the Jews in their prayers frequently ascribe to God (*Bech.* f. 71. c. 4. cd. *Rivæ di Trento*). He also teaches there that this Angel was the *Shekinah.* As does R. Joseph Gekatilia[41] in his book called *Saare Ora* (*Gates of Light*), according to Menasseh Ben Israel[42] (q. 64. in Gen. p. 118). Aben Sueb[43] on this place, a man of name among his party, writes much to the same purpose here as well.

These are followed by two eminent authors of the Cabalists. The one in his notes on the Zohar (f. 122) toward the end says, "*The Angel that delivered me from all evil is the Shekinah,*" is the one of whom it had said, "'*And the Angel of the Lord, who went before the camp of Israel, removed and went behind them;*" and may God bless us in the age to come" (Ex 14:19). The other is he who contracted the Zohar on Genesis and is called R. David

---

[41] Joseph ben Abraham Gikatilla (1248-1305). Spanish kabbalist.
[42] Born Manoel Dias Soeiro (1604-1657). Portuguese rabbi, kabbalist, writer, diplomat, and founded the first Hebrew printing press in Amsterdam in 1626. The book cited seems to be *Primo Questionum in Genesis*, previously published as *The Conciliator*.
[43] Joel ibn Shu'aib (15th cent). Spanish rabbi, preaching, commentator.

the Less.⁴⁴ In that book (*ed. Thessalonic.* f. 174), he professes to follow the opinion of R. Gekatalia in his *Saare Ora*.

Nor does Menasseh Ben Israel himself dissent much from these in the above-mentioned place. For though he attempts to reconcile Gen 48:16⁴⁵ with the First Commandment, "*You shall have no other gods before me*" (Ex 20:3), by saying it was the opinion of several of their masters that there was no contradiction between them. Yet he produces the opinion of the Cabalists at length, for the satisfaction of his readers, who possibly would not agree in former reasons drawn only from modern authorities.

I did not mention R. Levi ben Gersom's⁴⁶ opinion, who denies the Angel here spoken of to be a creature, but calls him the *Intellectus Agens*, because he seems to have borrowed this notion from the Arabian philosophers; nor is it commonly received by those of his religion. Many others might be added to these Jewish testimonies; but what I have already produced is, I think, very sufficient.

---

⁴⁴ Probably David ben Yom Tov ibn Bilia (c. 1300-1361). Portuguese Hebrew scholar, translator, philosopher, exegete, and poet who wrote *Me'or Enayim*, a commentary on the Pentateuch.

⁴⁵ The original reads 28:16. This is surely a typo, though a difficult one (xxviii vs. xlviii). See comments on R. Menasseh below.

⁴⁶ Better known as Gersonides or Magister Leo Hebraeus (1288-1344). French Jewish philosopher, Talmudist, Mathematician, physician, astronomer. Wrote several commentaries on Scripture.

SECT. V.

HAVING THUS SHOWED the opinions of the ancient Jews concerning Jacob's Angel, and that to this day the tradition is not quite worn out that exalts him above a created angel; I now proceed to the third question, the clearing of which will fully justify that opinion of the ancient Jews concerning this text.

And that is, whether this form of blessing is also a prayer? The soundest and most popular view of Jews and Christians agree, that we cannot worship angels without idolatry. This Maimonides[47] affirms, as I quoted him above; and the Protestants, as all men know, abhor this idolatry in the Roman Church.

I do therefore positively assert that these words contain a prayer to the Angel, as well as to God, for a blessing on his children. This the Jews cannot oppose, since Jonathan their paraphrast, and other writers after him, do commonly term this blessing *tephillah* or a *prayer*. For this reason, R. Menasseh thought it necessary to endeavor to reconcile this section of the prayer of Jacob with the First Commandment; which forbids angel-worship according to the Jews' interpretation (R. *Menach. de Reh. in Pent.* f. 97. c. 4).

It is true that Jacob's form of blessing does seem to proceed from him either as a wish or a prophecy: a

---

[47] Moses ben Maimon (1135-1204). Spanish born rabbi who become one of the most influential of all medieval Torah scholars.

wish, as if he had said, "Would to the Lord, God and his Angel would bless the lads." A prophecy, as if he had foretold that God and his Angel would in after-times fulfil what he now wished. But it might be both a wish and a prophecy, and notwithstanding be a direct prayer to God and the redeeming Angel. It is well known how the Jews commonly delivered their petitions to God in this form. And yet I cannot refrain from giving one instance to confirm it. You may read it in Numbers 6:22ff. *"And the Lord said to Moses, saying, Speak to Aaron and his sons, Thus shall you bless the children of Israel, and say, 'The Lord bless[48] you, and keep you: The Lord make his face shine upon you, and be gracious to you: The Lord lift up his countenance upon you, and give you peace.' And they shall invoke my name for the children of Israel* [so our translation is to be mended] *and I will bless them."* So that in plain terms the form of blessing here prescribed by God is called *invocation*.

I cannot therefore see what should hinder, but that we, after Jacob's example, may offer up our prayers to a created angel, supposing, as some do, that Jacob prayed for a blessing to such a kind of an angel. It is a necessary consequence that Bellarmine[49] and others of

---

[48] The margin has *ybrk* here. This word was seen earlier and is from Gen 48:16. It means "to bless," thus linking the two passages in the author's mind.

[49] Robert Bellarmine (1542 –1621). Italian Jesuit and Cardinal. He was an important figure in the Counter-Reformation and a proponent of the Council of Trent. Margin has the reference: De Sanct. Beat. 1.i.c.29. Corn. A. Lap. On Gen. xlviii.

his communion draw from this instance: holy Jacob invoked an angel, therefore it is not unlawful for the Protestants to do the like; therefore, one may worship others besides God; these things, he says, cannot be denied, unless you reckon prayer to be no act of worship, and not to be peculiar to God alone.

But let those who believe Jacob's Angel was a mere creature, as they do in that Church, rid themselves of these difficulties as well as they can. Let them try how to convince a Socinian[50] from Ephesians 1:2 and other places of Scripture, where worship is ascribed to Christ. The Socinian has his answer ready; he may wish and pray to Christ for grace, though he is not God, since he does no more than Jacob did, when he prayed for a blessing on his children to a mere angel.

I am more concerned for these Divines of the Reformed Church, who have given the same interpretation of Jacob's Angel with as the Papists, though they cannot be ignorant they therefore dissent from the divinity of the ancient Jews, and the Fathers of the Christian Church, and even the more learned and candid Romanists, such as Masius[51] was; I might add, (which perhaps they have not considered) though they therein

---

[50] Socinianism. Named for Italian theologian Fausto Sozzini (Lat: Faustus Socinus). It is nontrinitarian in its view of Christ and precursor to many forms of Unitarianism within Protestantism.
[51] Andreas Masius (1514-73). Catholic priest, humanist, and one of the first Europeans to specialize in the Syriac language.

contradict the whole strain of the New Testament (See *Mercerus ad Pagnini* Lexicon, p. 1254).

The intended shortness of this treatise will not permit me to enlarge on this subject. However, there is one thing I must not pass over, which ought to be taken into consideration by the less cautious divines. It is very certain that the God who appeared to Jacob in Bethel was the very God who fed Israel in the desert, and against whom the Israelites in the wilderness rebelled. The Apostle is express that he was Christ, whom the Jews tempted in the wilderness, i.e. he was the *Logos*, and not a mere angel (cf. 1Co 10:4). The Apostle takes it for granted; and it was a thing undisputed by the synagogue in his time. And indeed, unless this is allowed, St. Paul's reasoning in this chapter is trifling and groundless.

Well, what can Bellarmine say to this, he who asserts a created angel to be spoken of in Gen 48:16? He has forgotten what he said on that text when he comes to this place. He here strenuously urges it against the Socinians, to prove that Christ was then in being when the Jews tempted him in the wilderness. And since he owns in this place that Christ in his Divine nature was he who led Israel through the wilderness, who is sometimes called God, and sometimes an Angel, he inconsiderately grants what he had denied before, that the Angel who redeemed Jacob from all evil, being the same Angel that conducted Israel, was also God.

SECT. VI.

YOU SEE WHAT CONTRADICTIONS Bellarmine falls into, out of his zeal to promote the doctrine of *invocation of saints*. I wish there was not something as bad in our Divines, that carries them into the very same contradictions. The best I can say for their excuse is only this, they have not carefully attended to the style of the holy Scriptures. Two or three things therefore I will mention, which occur frequently in the Scripture, that I think would have suggested higher thoughts of this Angel to one that considered what he read.

He who considers how often our Lord Christ is called in the New Testament *the Spouse*, or *Husband of the Church*, and compares it with the same title that God appropriates to himself under the Old Testament estate, will make little doubt that it was the same Christ who was then married to Israel. By the same rule one may infer that our Lord Christ, in calling himself a Shepherd, had a respect to that title by which he is so often described in his dealings with Jacob and his posterity. This the older Jews were sensible of; and therefore, in both Genesis 48:15 and 49:24 where God is mentioned as a Shepherd, they understand it of the *Shekinah* or *Logos* (cf. R. Menachem de Rekanah, from the book *Habbahir in Pent*. f. 84. c. 2). Of this also the Jews in Christ's time were certainly not ignorant. For when they heard Christ liken himself in one of his sermons to *the Good Shepherd* (John 10), they immediately understand that he was claiming to be the Messiah, and therefore they took up stones to stone him. And then in the process of his discourse, to reinforce this claim, he made himself One with the Father.

As Christ called himself a Shepherd to show that he was the God who had fed Jacob and his posterity like sheep; so also is Christ most frequently represented in the New Testament under the notion of a Redeemer; intimating by this that he was the same redeeming Angel of whom Jacob had spoken. It was he who was called the *Angel of his Presence* (Isa 63:9), by whom God redeemed his ancient people; and he is also called the *Angel of the Covenant* (Mal 3:1), in the promise of his coming in the time of the Gospel.

Here I should have put an end to this tract, but there are two objections that lie in my way and seem to require some kind of an answer.

The first is taken from the doctrine of the Jews, who, many of them, expound this redeeming Angel by *Metatron*;[52] and *Metatron*, according to them, is a

---

[52] Metatron (*mttron*). No one quite knows the origin of this name. Sometimes called "lesser Yahweh," some have suggested the possibility that the "him" in Ex 23:21 ("because my name is within *him* [the Angel]" refers to Metatron, where the *ttr* in the word comes from *tetra*, the word for "four" in Greek, and a shorthand for the Tetragrammaton—YHWH (i.e. four letters). See Andrei A. Orlov, *The Etymology of the Name 'Metatron,"* in *The Enoch-Metatron Tradition* (TSAJ, 107; Tuebiingen: Mohr-Sieback, 2005). An excerpt is here (http://www.marquette.edu/maqom/metatronname.html#_ftnref24). See point #7: last accessed 8-30-2019.

created angel, or, as some say, none other than Enoch who was translated. On this there seems to be as many authorities against us as for us.

But let it be observed, 1. Though the Jews have several names of angels which are not mentioned in Scripture, yet they are all formed out of the names of God, according to the rules of their Kabbalah, and that with respect to the ten Sephiroth,[53] as Buxtorf[54] has noted (*Lex. Talm.* p. 828).

2. This is plain from the word *Actariel*, which is at the beginning of the Jewish forms of excommunication. This is derived from כתר (*ktr*)[55] the name of the first of the ten Sephiroth. From this, the Talmudists place Actariel upon the throne (Beracotb, f. 7. c. 1) and distinguish him from the ministering angels that stand before the throne. But I refer the curious reader that would know more of this to the ancient Jewish book entitled *Berith Menucha*, c. 1.[56]

3. This is no less plain of the Angel *Metatron*, who, as they say, was he who discoursed with Moses (Ex 3) and the Angel in whom God placed his name. So that

---

[53] In Kabbalah, Sephiroth are emanations that allow the Creator to create indirectly. Some think of them as intermediary states or stages somewhere between this Creator and all else that exists.

[54] Johannes Bustorf (1564-1629). Hebraist, professor of Hebrew at Basel (Switzerland), known as "Master of the Rabbis."

[55] V. Bartolocci, f. 1. Et 450.

[56] Berit Menuchah (Covenant of Rest) is a work of practical Kabbalah written down in the 14th century by Rabbi Abraham ben Isaac of Granada. It contains a system of theurgy which uses secret names of God and his emanations for spiritual and magical purposes.

they acknowledge that though it is formed from the Latin tongue, yet it expresses the same that the Hebrew word *Shaddai* does, as R. S. Jarchi[57] on Exodus 23 confesses. Now, St. Jerome on Ezekiel 1:24 notes that the Greek interpreters sometimes render God's name *Shaddai* by *Logos*, which leads us into the meaning of those ancient Jews who believed Shaddai and Metatron were the same.

4. The majority of the Jews are so far from believing *Metatron* is Enoch, that they believe him to be the Messiah, the *Logos* before his incarnation (our phrase), or in their words, the soul of the Messiah, which they look on as something between God and the angels, whom nothing separates from the living God (see Reuchlin,[58] 1.i. *de Cabala*, p. 651 where he proves *Metatron* to be the Messiah from their writings or, in short, take the confession of Menasseh ben Israel q. 6. in Gen 2).

Truly, if one would compare all those places of the Old Testament that mention the Angel, whom the later Jews call *Metatron*, he would find such properties belonging to this Angel as are incommunicable to a creature. And this shows that they who have departed in this point from the tradition of their fathers did it on this ground, because they were loath to acknowledge

---

[57] Shlomo Yitzchaki (1040-1105). Also known as Rashi, he was a medieval French rabbi and author of a commentary on the Tanakh.
[58] Johann Reuchlin (1455-1522). German humanist and Greek and Hebrew scholar. He wrote a treatise *On the Art of Kabbalah* (1517).

the Divinity of the Messiah, which seemed to be clear upon allowing *Metatron* to be the Messiah. They were more careful to defend their own prejudices than the opinions of the ancients.

II. Another objection is made from the place in Revelation 1:4. The words are these, "*John to the seven churches that are in Asia, grace be to you, and peace from him that was, and is, and is to come, and from the seven spirits that are before his throne; and from Jesus Christ, who is the faithful witness…*" John here seems to wish and pray for grace, not only from the Father, but also from the seven angels that are before the throne of God, and so Jesus Christ must be reckoned among the ministering spirits.

This place is indeed abused by those of the Romish Church to show that prayers may be lawfully directed to angels. And the Jews themselves have contributed to lead some people of note into this mistake. For, besides the four chief angels, whom they make to preside over the four armies of angels, which they have chiefly grounded on Ezekiel 1, they speak of seven other angels that were created before the rest, and that wait on God before the veil that divides them from the *Shekinah*.[59]

The hearing of these things so often repeated by the Jews has given occasion, I say, to some considerable Divines believing these seven to be proper angels, whom St. John mentions in his Revelation. But then,

---

[59] R. Eliezer, *in capit.* c. 4.

not apprehending how prayers could be offered to them, nor why the priority is given to them before Christ, they would not have John here to have spoken a prayer, but only to have wished grace on the seven churches; and this they thought was consistent enough with the angel-worship forbidden by St. Paul (Col 2:18) and even in this very book (Rev 19:10, 22:9).

But to shorten this matter, I altogether deny that St. John intended here any created angels. What then did he mean by them? Nothing else but the Holy Spirit, for whose most perfect power and grace on the seven churches he here makes supplication. For as Cyril on Zechariah 3:9: "The seven of them are very important." The number seven is always a mark of perfection in the thing to which it is applied. St. John therefore thought of no allusion to the Jewish opinion of seven angels, when he prayed for grace from the seven spirits before the throne; but had in his mind to express the far more plentiful effusion and more powerful efficacy of the Holy Spirit under the Gospel than under the Law, and his never-ceasing ministry for the good of the Church, for which purposes he has received a vicarious authority under God, immediately after Christ, as Tertullian speaks (*Against Praxeas* c. 13), and for this interpretation I have Justin Martyr (*Exhortation to the Greeks*) and St. Augustine on my side.

St. John's way of expressing himself is borrowed from Zechariah 3:9, where God is represented as having seven eyes running through the earth, to signify by this symbol God's perfect knowledge of all things, as Cyril of Alexander notes. Hence, we read of Christ (Rev 3:1), *"The words of him who has the seven spirits of God."* And in another place seven eyes and seven horns are ascribed to him. But we never read (which is worth our observation) of these seven spirits as we do of the four beasts and twenty-four elders, that they fell down and worshipped God.

But why does St. John put the Holy Spirit before Christ? If I should say St. Paul has done something similar in Galatians 1:1 and Ephesians 5:5 (putting the Son before the Father) to teach us the unity and equality of each Person in the blessed Trinity, or because St. John in the following verses was to speak more at large of Christ, I think I should not answer improperly. But I shall add another reason, which may explain the whole matter.

In a word, I do believe this difficulty must be resolved another way; for that which makes this place so intricate according to the judgment of many interpreters is their referring to the Father the words of Revelation 1:4, *"Grace to you, and peace from him who is and who was and who is to come."* This ought to be referred particularly to Christ himself, who is described in 4:8 according to the description of the *Logos* in Jonathan's Targum on Deuteronomy 32:39. But then some will say, why is there any mention made of the seven spirits, if we conceive that the grace which is asked for the Church, in the first words, is asked from Jesus Christ? The thing is so clear that Socinus has perceived it.

Seven spirits are here mentioned to denote the Spirit of God, who was to reside with his sevenfold gifts in the Messiah, according to the prophecy of Isaiah 11:2-3. From here it comes that in Rev 5:6, the Lamb is described having seven horns and seven eyes, which are the seven spirits of God, sent forth into all the earth. To Christ there are attributed seven horns, which denote his empire, in opposition to the empire of the little horn, which is spoken of (Dan 7:8). So there are seven eyes, which are the seven spirits of God, attributed to him; likewise, to denote the gracious providence of Jesus Christ by the Holy Ghost, and that in opposition to the little horn, in which there were eyes, *"like the eyes of man"* (Dan 7:8).

Here then *the grace asked* is from the seven spirits, that is, from the Holy Ghost, who is united in one with the Messiah Jesus Christ, and is sent by him; and so it is said to be asked from Jesus Christ himself, who both has those spirits as his eyes and does cause the mission of them to his Church.

St. John therefore does not place the Holy Spirit before Christ, but mentions him with Christ, because after Christ's ascension and during the time of Christ's continuance to God's right hand, he has a more particular hand in the immediate government of the Church, and is especially watchful to do her good. For this reason, I think it is that the Holy Spirit is placed as it were without the veil, like a ministering angel. Many of the ancients knew this, as Victorinus of Pettau, Ambrose, Bede, Arethas,[60] Autpert Ambrose, Walafrid Strabo, Haymo,[61] Rupertus,[62] from whom Thomas Aquinas, and Cælius of Pannonia,[63] who rebukes those that understand it otherwise, and other elder Divines of the Roman Church learnt it, to say nothing of those of the Reformed Church: but it is time now to be finished.

---

[60] Probably the ninth century Arethas of Caesarea rather than the 6th century martyr.
[61] Probably the 9th century Haymo of Halberstadt rather than the 13th century Haymo of Faversham.
[62] Probably Rupert of Deutz (1075-1129) rather than Rupert of Bingen (712-732) or Rupert of Salzburg (660-710).
[63] Allix may refer here to Gregory Bánffy (d. 1545), also called Caelius Pannonius. He was a Hungarian from the Paulist order who wrote on Revelation and the Song of Songs.

Commentaries on Genesis 48:15-16

Jewish

And I said to Him, "I pray, O Lord, tell me Your name, that I may call upon You in a day of tribulation." And He said, "I am the Angel who intercedes for the race of Israel, that He smite them not utterly, because every evil spirit attacks it". And after these things I was as it were awakened, and blessed the Most High and the Angel that intercedes for the race of Israel, and for all the righteous [Gen 48:16].

(Testament of Levi 5:5-6)[64]

---

[64] Alexander Roberts, James Donaldson, and A. Cleveland Coxe, eds., "The Testaments of the Twelve Patriarchs," in *The Ante-Nicene Fathers: Fathers of the Third and Fourth Centuries: The Twelve Patriarchs, Excerpts and Epistles, the Clementina, Apocrypha, Decretals, Memoirs of Edessa and Syriac Documents, Remains of the First Ages*, trans. R. Sinker, vol. 8 (Buffalo, NY: Christian Literature Company, 1886), 13.

"*The Angel that delivered me from all evil*" is the Shekinah, of whom Ex 24:19 says, "*And the Angel of the Lord, who went before the camp of Israel, removed and went behind them;*" and may God bless us in the age to come."

(The Zohar)[65]

According to R. Moses of Gerona, the command of God not to serve other gods, is, not to worship any terrestrial, celestial, or angelic creatures; as it would be a species of idolatry, although intended for the First Cause. If this is so, how did Jacob come to address a prayer to the Angel?

Reconciliation ... Or, according to the idea of the Cabalistic theologians, it may be considered otherwise. We know that according to Maimonides, the fifth of the thirteen articles of Faith is that prayer and worship must be addressed to the First Cause alone, and to no angel or sovereign creatures; consequently not to place an intermediator between God and man, because He alone acts voluntarily with infinite power—will and power being united in Him; besides, Israel, as the peculiar people of God, are not subjected to, or under the influence of the planets, and ought not to address or direct their prayers, but to the First Cause only, as the ancient sages taught from these words, "What nation is so great whom God is so near to as the Lord our God, in all things we call on him for;" so that we ought to

---

[65] F. 122, as quoted by Allix.

call on him, and not on angels (as Michael or Gabriel); according to this, there seems a difficulty in what the same theologians say, that when a man offers up prayers his intention should be directed to a certain Sephira.[66] The Sephirot being the ten lights or attributes emanating from the First Cause, this interposition seems contrary to the maxim of Maimonides; but in order to comprehend it, it must be stated that these Sephirot or ten sovereign lights (this being the number, as the Cabalists have received traditionally) emanate from the First Cause, and are therefore rays of his Divinity—and Divine influence is diffused into them: and as the Lord is immutable, when He acts mercifully, it is said He acts by the Sephira called *hesed* (mercy); when rigorously just, by *gibborah* (might). Therefore, the Cabalists saying that the intention must be directed to a certain Sephira, means to that attribute of the First Cause through whose means he operates. So R. Nehunia ben Acana, in the prayer he composed for the order of the ten Sephirot, says "Beautify yourself in the first

---

[66] See note 53 above. This argument is very important to understand properly. Throughout the ages, Greeks, Christians, and Jews alike who believe in a simple, undivided divine essence have had to figure out ways of speaking of this God acting in creation. Sometimes they said it was through his Power (which becomes personified). Other times they say it is through his Logos or Son. Sometimes they say any such language it is pure anthropomorphism. Here, the Kabbalists argue that it is through the Sephira or emanations (not to be confused with Gnosticism, though the ideas certainly overlap). The point he is making, as is clear at the end of the quote, is that in no way do the Kabbalists argue that worship is being given to anyone but God. Yet, Jacob is worshiping the angel.

Sephira"; he does not say beautify *the* first Sephira, but *in* the first Sephira, that is addressing the First Cause as acting through it...

In conclusion, it is to be said that Jacob prayed to the First Cause, and addressed in the highest perfection the intention to the means by which he prayed He would act ... he began with *elohim* (God), and finished with *melek* (angel), which is the Shekinah ... What has been stated is solely for the purpose of undeceiving those, who, from the being unacquainted with Cabala, might suppose that those theologians address their prayer to any of those lights or sovereign creatures, the contrary being the case as has been most clearly demonstrated.

(Manasseh ben Israel)[67]

"*The redeeming Angel,*" he says, is he that answered him in the time of his affliction, and who said to him, "*I am the God of Bethel,*" etc. "*he,*" of whom it is said, that "*my name* is in him." He says the same thing on Exodus 3 where the appearance in the bush is mentioned: "*This is he of whom it is said, and God called Moses out of the bush.*" He is called an Angel, because he governs the world; for it is written in one place, And "*Jehovah,*" that is, the "*Lord God, brought us out of Egypt;*" and in another place, "*He sent his Angel and brought us out of Egypt.*" And again, "*The Angel of his presence saved*

---

[67] Question 67 on Genesis 48:16 in *The Conciliator of R. Manasseh Ben Israel: A Reconcilement of the Apparent Contradictions in Holy Scripture*, vol. 1 (London: Duncan and Malcolm, 1842), 90-93.

them," viz. that Angel who is the face of God, of whom it is said, "*My face shall go before you.*" Lastly, that Angel of whom the prophet Malachi mentions, "*And the Lord whom you seek shall suddenly come to his temple, even the Angel of the covenant, whom you desire.*" At length he adds, "The face of God is God himself, as all interpreters do acknowledge; but none can rightly understand this, without being instructed in the mysteries of the Law."

(R. Moses Ben Nachman)[68]

He means the Shekinah, says he, when he speaks of the redeeming Angel.

(R. Menachem of Rekan)[69]

---

[68] Moses ben Nahman (1194-1270). As quoted by Allix.
[69] F. 52. See also f. 55. Quoted by Allix.

Christian Interpretations

(15) And yet, even after all these arguments, Scripture rightly does not cease to call an angel God, and God an angel. (16) When this same Jacob was about to bless Manasseh and Ephraim, the sons of Joseph, he placed his hands crosswise upon the heads of the boys and said: "May God who has nourished me from my youth even to this day, the angel who has delivered me from all evils, bless the boys." (17) So conclusively does he affirm that the same one whom he had called God is an angel that he does not hesitate towards the end of his sentence to place the person of whom he was speaking in the singular number, saying: "May He bless these boys." (18) For if he had meant the angel to be taken as a separate person, he would have joined two persons together in the plural number; instead he used the singular number for one person in the blessing. Consequently, he wished the same person to be considered God and angel. (19) Although God the Father cannot be considered to be an angel, Christ can readily be taken to be both God and angel.

(Novatian)[70]

---

[70] Novatian, *The Trinity, The Spectacles, Jewish Foods, In Praise of Purity, Letters*, ed. Hermigild Dressler, trans. Russell J. DeSimone, vol. 67, The Fathers of the Church (Washington, DC: The Catholic University of America Press, 1974), 75–76.

None of created and natural Angels did [Jacob] join to God their Creator, nor rejecting God that fed him, did he from any Angel ask the blessing on his grandsons; but in saying, "*Who delivered me from all evil*," he showed that it was no created Angel, but the Word of God, whom he joined to the Father in his prayer, through whom, whomsoever He will, God does deliver. For knowing that He is also called the Father's "*Angel of great Counsel*," (Isa 9:6 LXX) he said that none other than He was the Giver of blessing, and Deliverer from evil.

(Athanasius)[71]

Despite having obvious indications of God's favor for him, he kept his soul humble in saying, "*O God, before whom my forebears Abraham and Isaac were pleasing.*" Then he said, "*You who have nourished me from my youth to this day.*" Notice in this, once again, the extraordinary degree of his gratitude. Instead of mentioning his own virtue, he narrates God's doings to him in saying, "*You who have nourished me from my youth to this day.*" In other words, You who personally managed my affairs from the beginning until the present. Likewise he had said previously, "*I crossed the Jordan with only my staff and, lo,*

---

[71] Athanasius of Alexandria (296-373), "Four Discourses against the Arians" 3.12, in *St. Athanasius: Select Works and Letters*, ed. Philip Schaff and Henry Wace, trans. John Henry Newman and Archibald T. Robertson, vol. 4, A Select Library of the Nicene and Post-Nicene Fathers of the Christian Church, Second Series (New York: Christian Literature Company, 1892), 400.

I have now become two camps." Now he says the same thing in different words, *"You who have nourished me from my youth to this day, the angel who has snatched me from all my troubles."*

(Chrysostom)[72]

This Angel is that Lord or Son of God whom Jacob saw and who was to be sent by God into the world to announce to us deliverance from death, the forgiveness of sins, and the kingdom of heaven ... Therefore, one must note carefully that Jacob is speaking about Christ, the Son, who alone is the Angel or Ambassador ... not the Father, not the Holy Spirit. For he makes a clear distinction among the three Persons. Yet he adds: *"May He bless these lads."*

(Martin Luther)[73]

He so joins the Angel to God as to make him his equal. Truly he offers him divine worship and asks the same things from him as from God. If this is understood indifferently of any angel whatever, the sentence is absurd. ... It is necessary that Christ should be here

---

[72] John Chrysostom, *Homilies on Genesis 46–67*, ed. Thomas P. Halton, trans. Robert C. Hill, vol. 87, The Fathers of the Church (Washington, DC: The Catholic University of America Press, 1992), 260–261.

[73] Martin Luther (1483-1546), *Luther's Works, Vol. 8: Lectures on Genesis: Chapters 45-50*, ed. Jaroslav Jan Pelikan, Hilton C. Oswald, and Helmut T. Lehmann, vol. 8 (Saint Louis: Concordia Publishing House, 1999), 163-64.

meant, who does not bear in vain the title of Angel, because he had become the perpetual Mediator. ... He had not yet indeed been sent by the Father, to approach more nearly to us by taking our flesh, but because he was always the bond of connection between God and man ... there was always so wide a distance between God and men, that, without a mediator, there could be no communication ... and because God formally manifested himself in no other way than through him, he is properly called the Angel."

(John Calvin)[74]

Gen 48:16. "*Let the angel that kept me bless your children.*" Here (say they) it is a prayer made to angels. *Ans.* By the angel is meant Christ, who is called the angel of the covenant (Mal 3:1) and the angel that guided Israel in the wilderness (1Co 10:9 compared with Ex 23:20).

(William Perkins)[75]

V. 16. *Angel.* Christ, the Angel of the covenant (Mal 3:1). The Angel in whom God's name is (Ex 23:20-21).

---

[74] John Calvin (1509-1564) and John King, *Commentary on the First Book of Moses Called Genesis*, vol. 2 (Bellingham, WA: Logos Bible Software, 2010), 428-29.

[75] William Perkins (1558-1602), *A Golden Chaine: Or The Description of Theologie Containing the Order of the Causes of Saluation and Damnation, according to Gods Word. A View Whereof Is to Be Seene in the Table Annexed. Hereunto Is Adioyned the Order Which M. Theodore Beza Vsed in Comforting Afflicted Consciences*, Early English Books Online (Cambridge: John Legat, printer to the Vniuersitie of Cambridge, 1600), 988.

Called here Jacobs' Redeemer, or Deliverer, which is the title of God (Ps 19:15; Isa 43:14 and 47:4). The Rabbis acknowledge this Angel to be God, saying; "He mentions also God's majesty (Shekinah) when he says, '*The Angel that redeemed me*' (R. Menachem on Gen 48. See also Gen. 31:11).

(Henry Ainsworth)[76]

V. 16. *The Angel.* The son of God who appeared in the time of the fathers, and in whom the everlasting Father did manifest himself to them, as in the person of the mediator (see upon Genesis 16:7) and is the same who was called "*God*" in the previous verse.

(Giovani Diodati)[77]

IV. But neither Saint nor Angel must be adored or called upon religiously. Because 1. for this we have neither precept, nor example, nor promise in Scripture. 2. By invocating the Saints, we make them omniscient and omnipotent, which are only God's attributes. 3. Because we must not believe in the Saints. "*Now how shall they call on him in whom they have not believed*" (Rom 10:14)? 4. Because they refused religious worship by the example of Peter (Acts 10:25, 26), and of the Angel (Rev 19:10, 22:8). The objections of Papists are

---

[76] Henry Ainsworth (1571-1622), *Annotations Upon the First Book of Moses, Called Genesis* (n.p., 1616), comments on Genesis 48:16.
[77] Giovani Diodati (1576-1649), *Pious Annotations Upon the Holy Bible Expounding the Difficult Places Thereof* (London: Nicolas Fussell, 1643), 33.

frivolous, for that saying in Gen 48:16 is to be understood not of a created, but of an uncreated, Angel, that is the Son of God (Gen 48:16).

(John Wolleb [Wollebius])[78]

"The Angel which redeemed me from all evil bless the lads…" The fountain of blessing is described by another name, the Angel which can be no other but God, in whose name he blesses and God in Christ the Angel of the Covenant.

(George Hughes)[79]

Bellarmine's allegation for the invocation of angels, from Jacob's practice (Gen 48:16) is refuted by the context, because it is interpreted in such a grammatical way that it is against the theological and logical sense of the words, that is, in such a sense as is against the analogy of religion in the Decalogue (which is as necessarily observed in the interpretation of doubtful propositions in the Old, as the analogy of faith is in the New Testament) and against the analogy of reason,

---

[78] Johannes Wolleb (1589-1629), *The Abridgment of Christian Divinitie so Exactly and Methodically Compiled That It Leads Us as It Were by the Hand to the Reading of the Holy Scriptures, Ordering of Common-Places, Understanding of Controversies, Clearing of Some Cases of Conscience / by John Wollebius; Faithfully Translated into English … by Alexander Ross*, Early English Books Online (London: T. Mabb for Joseph Nevill and are to be sold at his shop.., 1660), 353.

[79] George Hughes (1603-1667), *An Analytical Exposition of the Whole First Book of Moses, Called Genesis* (n.p., 1673), 574.

both in the proposition, and in the connection, and in the deduction.

(Edward Hyde)[80]

The angel of the covenant, in whom is the name of God, that hath power of pardoning or retaining transgressions,—Jesus Christ, the angel who redeems his out of all their troubles, Gen 48:16,—he is in the midst of them, and amongst them.

11. Second, he is called an "*Angel*" by Jacob himself. "*The Angel that redeemed me*" (Gen 48:16). This was the greatest danger that Jacob was ever in, and this he remembers in his blessing of Joseph's children, praying that they may have the presence of this Angel with them, who preserved him all his life, and delivered him from that imminent danger from his brother Esau. And he calls him, "*The Angel the Redeemer;*" which is the name of the promised Messiah, as the Jews grant, "*And the Goël* (the 'Redeemer') *shall come to Zion*" (Isa 59:20). He is also expressly called "*The Angel*" in Hosea 12:4.

---

[80] Edward Hyde (1607-1659), *A Christian Vindication of Truth against Errour Concerning These Controversies, 1. Of Sinners Prayers, 2. Of Priests Marriage, 3. Of Purgatory, 4. Of the Second Commandment and Images, 5. Of Praying to Saints and Angels, 6. Of Justification by Faith, 7. Of Christs New Testament or Covenant / by Edw. Hide*, Early English Books Online (London: R. White for Richard Davis .., 1659), 245–246.

12. Third, this man in appearance, this Angel in office, was in name and nature God over all, blessed forever. For, in the first place, Jacob prays solemnly to him for his blessing (Gen 32:26), and refuses to let him go, or to cease his appeals, until he had blessed him. He does so, he blesses him, and gives him a double pledge or token of it, in the touch of his thigh and change of his name; giving him a name to denote his prevailing with God—that is, with himself. From this, Jacob concludes that he had "*seen God*," and calls the name of the place, "*The face of God.*" In the second place, Genesis 48:16, besides that he invokes this Angel for his presence with and blessing on the children of Joseph,—which cannot regard any but God himself without gross idolatry—it is evident that "the Angel who redeemed him" (16) is the same with "*the God who fed him,*" that is, the God of his fathers.

(John Owen)[81]

Our main support in this sinking condition is, that Christ appears for us, and lives to do it. He is concerned for his people when they are in the depths, he has always been so, Gen 48:16. This angel is Christ, who redeemed him. The word is גאל (*Goel*), the Redeemer, as Christ is

---

[81] The first quote is John Owen (1616-1683), *The Works of John Owen*, ed. William H. Goold, vol. 8 (Edinburgh: T&T Clark, n.d.), 154. The second is from Owen's Exercitation 10 in the first volume of his Hebrew's commentary. I have reprinted this exercitation as a separate volume in this series on Christ in All Scripture.

called (Job 19:25; Isa 59:20). He redeemed Jacob not only from eternal miseries but delivered him out of all the troubles and calamites he had met with in the world.

(David Clarkson)[82]

Jacob mentions three times the God from whom he seeks a blessing for his sons: "*God, before whom my fathers did walk; the God which fed me all my life long unto this day, the Angel which redeemed me from all evil, bless the lads*" (Gen 48:15, 16). Now the angel who redeemed him from all evil and from whom he sought the blessing could not be a creature. Here also must be referred the *seraphic trisagion*: "Holy, holy, holy is Jehovah God of Hosts" (Isa 6:3).

(Francis Turretin)[83]

The Angel; not surely a created angel, but Christ Jesus, who is called an *Angel* (Ex 23:20), and *the Angel of the covenant* (Mal 3:1), who was the conductor of the Israelites in the wilderness, as plainly appears by comparing of Ex 23:20-21 with 1Co 10:4, 9. Add to this that this Angel is called Jacob's *Redeemer*, which is the title appropriated by God to himself (Isa 43:14; 47:4), and that *from all evil*, and therefore from sin, from which no

---

[82] David Clarkson (1622-1686), *The Works of David Clarkson*, vol. 3 (Edinburgh: James Nichol, 1864), 163.
[83] Francis Turretin (1623-1687), *Institutes of Elenctic Theology*, ed. James T. Dennison Jr., trans. George Musgrave Giger, vol. 1 (Phillipsburg, NJ: P&R Publishing, 1992–1997), 276.

created angel can deliver us, but Christ only (Matt 1:21); and that Jacob worships and prays to this Angel no less than to God for the blessing, and that without any note of distinction, the word *bless* being in the singular number, and equally relating to God and to the Angel; and that the Angel to whom he here ascribes his deliverances from all evil, must in all reason be the same to whom he prayed for these very deliverances which he here commemorates, and that was no other than the very *God of Abraham*, as is evident from Gen 28:15, 20, 21; 32:9–11; 35:3.

(Matthew Poole)[84]

Nor ought it to be urged that the Son, even before his incarnation, was called מלאך (*malak*) the Angel (Gen 48:16; Ex 23:20). For that signifies no inferiority of the Son before the time appointed for his incarnation; but only a form resembling the appearances of angels, and prefiguring his future mission into the world.

(Herman Witsius)[85]

He had by his angel *redeemed him from all evil*, v. 16. A great deal of hardship he had known in his time, but God had graciously kept him from the evil of his

---

[84] Matthew Poole (1624-1679), *Annotations upon the Holy Bible*, vol. 1 (New York: Robert Carter and Brothers, 1853), 107.
[85] Herman Witsius (1636-1708), *The Economy of the Covenants between God and Man: Comprehending a Complete Body of Divinity*, trans. William Crookshank, vol. 1 (London: T. Tegg & Son, 1837), 151.

troubles. Now that he was dying, he looked upon himself as *redeemed from all evil*, and bidding an everlasting farewell to sin and sorrow. Christ, the Angel of the covenant, is he that redeems us from all evil, 2Ti 4:18.

(Matthew Henry)[86]

The Angel which redeemed me from all evil, bless the lads, etc. ... this is not to be understood of a created angel he wishes to be their guardian, but of an uncreated one, the Son of God, the Angel of God's presence, the Angel of the covenant; the same with the God of his father before mentioned, as appears by the character he gives him, as having redeemed him *from all evil;* not only protected and preserved him from temporal evils and imminent dangers from Esau, Laban, and others; but had delivered him from the power, guilt, and punishment of sin, the greatest of evils, and from the dominion and tyranny of Satan the evil one, and from everlasting wrath, ruin, and damnation; all which none but a divine Person could do, as well as he wishes, desires, and prays, that he would *bless* the lads with blessings temporal and spiritual, which a created angel cannot do; and Jacob would never have asked it of him:

(John Gill)[87]

---

[86] Matthew Henry (1662-1714), *Matthew Henry's Commentary on the Whole Bible: Complete and Unabridged in One Volume* (Peabody: Hendrickson, 1994), 90.

[87] John Gill (1697-1771), *An Exposition of the Old Testament*, vol. 1, The Baptist Commentary Series (London: Mathews and Leigh, 1810), 298.

The scriptures they bring in defense of this practice are nothing to their purpose. For whenever an angel is said to intercede for men, as when it is said, "*The angel of the Lord answered and said, O Lord of hosts, how long will you not have mercy on Jerusalem, and on the cities of Judah?*" or to be the object of their prayers or supplications, as Jacob says, "*The angel which redeemed me from all evil, bless the lads,*" no other person is intended but Christ, "*the Angel of the covenant.*"

(Thomas Ridgley)[88]

The word angel etymologically signifies messenger. But by the universally received usage and style of Scripture language it designates a nature and a specific creature. Yet because the word is originally nothing more than a designation of office, it is used in the Scriptures with reference also to the Son of God, as the uncreated angel (Isa 63:9; Mal 3:1; Gen 48:16, etc.). Also with reference to men (Mal 2:7; Rev 1:20; Mal 3:1; Mark 1:2; Matt 11:10; Luke 7:27).

(Heinrich Schmid)[89]

---

[88] Thomas Ridgley (1667-1734), *A Body of Divinity*, vol. 1 (New York: Robert Carter & Brothers, 1855), 472.
[89] Heinrich Schmid (1811-1886), *The Doctrinal Theology of the Evangelical Lutheran Church, Verified from the Original Sources*, trans. Charles A. Hay and Henry E. Jacobs, Second English Edition, Revised according to the Sixth German Edition. (Philadelphia, PA: Lutheran Publication Society, 1889), 207.

The 2nd person seems to be identified in the following places: Gen 16:7, *the Angel of Jehovah found Hagar*—v. 10, He promises to exert divine power—v. 11, claims to have heard her distress; and v. 13, Hagar is surprised that she survives the Divine vision. Gen 18, three men visit Abraham identified as angels (19:1). The chief angel of these three, in 18:1, 14, 17, &c., makes Himself known as Jehovah, receives Abraham's worship, &c. And in Gen 48:15, 16, this Jehovah is called by Jacob, "*the Angel which redeemed me from all evil,*" etc., and invoked to bless Joseph's sons, a divine function. Again, in Gen 21:17, The Angel of God speaks to Hagar, promising her, v. 18, a divine exertion of power. In Gen 22:1, אֱלוֹהִים commands Abraham to take his son Isaac and sacrifice him. Vs. 11, when in the act of doing it, the Angel of Jehovah arrests, and says, "*You have not withheld your son from me*" (13); and Abraham names the place Jehovah Jireh (14). In Gen 31:11, the Angel of Jehovah appears to Jacob in a dream, identified in vs. 13, with God, the God of Gen 28:11–22, the God of Bethel then declared Jehovah. In Gen 32:25, Jacob wrestles with an angel, seeks his blessing, and names the place *Peniel* (30). This Angel is in the narrative called Elohim, and Hosea 12:4–6, describing the same transaction, Elohim, Angel and Jehovah of Hosts. In the same method compare Ex 3:2, with vs. 4, 6, 14–16; Ex 14:19, with vs. 24; Ex 23:20, with subsequent verse; Ex 32:34; Num 22:22, with vv. 32–35; Josh 5:13 to

6:2; Jdg 2:1–4. Compare Jdg 6:11-22; Jdg 13:3, with vs. 21, 22. And Isa 63:9; Zech 1:12–15, compare 6:15. Compare Zech 3:2, with 5:1; Ps 34:7; 35:5.

(R. L. Dabney)[90]

All the divine appearances of the ancient economy are referred to *one person*.—Compare Gen 18:2, 17; 28:13; 32:9, 31; Ex 3:14, 15; 13:21; 20:1, 2; 25:21; Deut 4:33, 36, 39; Neh 9:7–28. This one person is called Jehovah, the incommunicable name of God, and at the same time *angel*, or *one sent*.—Compare Gen 31:11, 13; 48:15, 16; Hos 12:2, 5. Compare Ex 3:14, 15, with Acts 7:30–35; and Ex 13:21, with Ex 14:19; and Ex 20:1, 2, with Acts 7:38; Isa 63:7, 9.

But God the Father has been seen by no man (John 1:18; 6:46): neither could he be an angel, or one sent by any other; yet God the Son has been seen (1Jn 1:1, 2), and sent (John 5:36).

(A. A. Hodge)[91]

III. THE ANGEL OF THE COVENANT

… Having therefore identified the Messiah with the angel of the covenant, it only remains to show that

---

[90] R. L. Dabney (1820-1898), *Syllabus and Notes of the Course of Systematic and Polemic Theology*, Second Edition. (St. Louis: Presbyterian Publishing Company, 1878), 188.
[91] Archibald Alexander Hodge (1823-1886), *Outlines of Theology: Rewritten and Enlarged* (New York: Hodder & Stoughton, 1878), 170.

this was a divine angel, having the names, attributes and authority of God, and receiving the worship peculiar to him alone.

1. *Divine names* are given to him and claimed by him.

(1) That of JEHOVAH. By the inspired writers: Gen 16:13; 18:1, 17, 20, 26, 33; Ex 3:4, 7 (cf. ver. 2); 13:21 (cf. with Ex 14:19); Josh 5:13 (cf. with 6:2).

(2) That of GOD. By Hagar, Gen 16:13; by Jacob, Gen 32:30; 48:15, 16; by the writer, Ex 3:4, 6; by God himself, Gen 31:13 (cf. vs. 11; also ch. 28:13–22 and 32:9); Ex 3:2, 6.

(James P. Boyce)[92]

(*a*) The angel of Jehovah identifies himself with Jehovah; (*b*) he is identified with Jehovah by others; (*c*) he accepts worship due only to God. Though the phrase "angel of Jehovah" is sometimes used in the later Scriptures to denote a merely human messenger or created angel, it seems in the Old Testament, with hardly more than a single exception, to designate the pre-incarnate Logos, whose manifestations in angelic or human form foreshadowed his final coming in the flesh.

(*a*) Gen 22:11, 16—"*the angel of Jehovah called unto him* [Abraham, when about to sacrifice Isaac]... *By myself have I sworn, with Jehovah*"; 31:11, 13—"*the angel of*

---

[92] James Petigru Boyce (1827-1888), *Abstract of Systematic Theology* (Bellingham, WA: Logos Bible Software, 2010), 267–268.

God said unto me [Jacob].... I am the God of Beth-el." (b) Gen 16:9, 13—*"angel of Jehovah said unto her ... and she called the name of Jehovah that spoke unto her, You are a God who sees"*; 48:15, 16—*"the God who fed me ... the angel who hath redeemed me."*

(Augustus Strong)[93]

It is another question, however, whether there may not exist in the pages of the Old Testament turns of expression or records of occurrences in which one already acquainted with the doctrine of the Trinity may fairly see indications of an underlying implication of it. The older writers discovered intimations of the Trinity in such phenomena as the plural form of the Divine name *Ĕlōhīm*, the occasional employment with reference to God of plural pronouns (*"Let us make man in our image,"* Gen 1:26; 3:22; 11:7; Isa 6:8), or of plural verbs (Gen 20:13; 35:7), certain repetitions of the name of God which seem to distinguish between God and God (Ps 45:6, 7; 105:1; Hos 1:7), threefold liturgical formulas Num 6:24, 26; Isa 6:3), a certain tendency to hypostatize the conception of Wisdom (Prov 8), and especially the remarkable phenomena connected with the appearances of the Angel of Jehovah (Gen 16:2–13, 22:11, 16; 31:11, 13; 48:15, 16; Ex 3:2, 4, 5; Jdg 13:20–22) ... After all is said, in the light of

---

[93] Augustus Hopkins Strong (1836-1921), *Systematic Theology* (Philadelphia: American Baptist Publication Society, 1907), 319.

the later revelation, the Trinitarian interpretation remains the most natural one of the phenomena which the older writers frankly interpreted as intimations of the Trinity; especially of those connected with the descriptions of the Angel of Jehovah no doubt.

(B. B. Warfield)[94]

God does not appear only in impersonal signs, however, but also visits his people in personal beings ... Among all these envoys of God the Messenger of the Lord (מלאך יהוה) occupies a special place. He appears to Hagar (Gen 16:6–13; 21:17–20); to Abraham (Gen 18; 19; 22; 24:7; 40); to Jacob (Gen 28:13–17; 31:11–13; 32:24–30; cf. Hos 12:4; Gen 48:15, 16); to, and at the time of, Moses (Ex 3:2f.; 13:21; 14:19; 23:20–23; 32:34; 33:2f.; cf. Num 20:16; Isa 63:8, 9; and further also Josh 5:13, 14; Jdg 6:11–24; 13:2–23). This *Malak YHWH* is not an independent symbol nor a created angel but a true personal revelation and appearance of God, distinct from him (Ex 23:20–23; 33:14f.; Isa 63:8, 9) and still one with him in name (Gen 16:13; 31:13; 32:28, 30; 48:15, 16; Ex 3:2f.; 23:20–23; Jdg 13:3), in power (Gen 16:10, 11; 21:18; 18:14, 18; Ex 14:19; Jdg 6:21), in redemption and blessing (Gen 48:16; Ex 3:8; 23:20; Isa 63:8, 9), in adoration and honor (Gen 18:3; 22:12; Ex 23:21) ... The angel of the

---

[94] Benjamin B. Warfield (1851-1921), *The Works of Benjamin B. Warfield: Biblical Doctrines*, vol. 2 (Bellingham, WA: Logos Bible Software, 2008), 140-41.

covenant again appears in prophecy (Zech 1:8–12:3) and will come to his temple (Mal 3:1). Theophany reaches its climax, however, in Christ who is the ἀγγελος, δοξα, εἰκων, λογος, υἱος του θεου (Angel, Glory, Image, Word, Son of God) in whom God is fully revealed and fully given.

(Herman Bavinck)[95]

The most important and characteristic form of revelation in the patriarchal period is that through "the Angel of Jehovah" or "the Angel of God." The references are: Gen 16:7; 22:11, 15; 24:7, 40; 31:11; 48:16 [cp. also Hos 12:4, with reference to Gen 32:24ff.].

The peculiarity in all these cases is that, on the one hand, the Angel distinguishes himself from Jehovah, speaking of Him in the third person, and that, on the other hand, in the same utterance he speaks of God in the first person. Of this phenomenon various explanations have been offered … We must assume that behind the twofold representation there lies a real manifoldness in the inner life of the Deity. If the Angel sent were Himself partaker of Godhead, then He could refer to God as his sender, and at the same time speak as God, and in both cases there would be reality behind it. Without this much of what we call the Trinity, the

---

[95] Herman Bavinck (1854-1921), John Bolt, and John Vriend, *Reformed Dogmatics: Prolegomena*, vol. 1 (Grand Rapids, MI: Baker Academic, 2003), 328–330.

transaction could not but have been unreal and illusory.

(Geerhardus Vos)[96]

3. The "angel of the LORD" who is both *identified* as God and yet *differentiated* from God (Gen 16:7–13; 22:1–2, 11–18; 24:7, 40; 28:10–17 and 31:11–13; 32:9–12, 24–30; 48:15–16; Ex 3:2–6; 13:21 and 14:19; 23:20–23 and 33:14; 32:34; Josh 5:13–15; Jdg 6:11–24; 13:3–22; 2Sa 24:16; Hos 12:4; Zech 12:8; and Mal 3:1).

(Robert Reymond)[97]

The mysterious "angel of the LORD" or "angel of God," who appears often in the early Old Testament story and is sometimes identified with the God from whom he is at other times distinguished (Gen 16:7–13; 18:1–33; 22:11–18; 24:7, 40; 31:11–13; 32:24–30; 48:15–16; Ex 3:2–6; 14:19; 23:20–23; 32:34–33:5; Num 22:22–35; Josh 5:13–15; Jdg 2:1–5; 6:11–23; 9:13–23), is in some sense God acting as his own messenger, and is commonly seen as a preincarnate appearance of God the Son.

(J. I. Packer)[98]

---

[96] Geerhardus Vos (1862-1949), *Biblical Theology: Old and New Testaments* (Eugene, OR: Wipf & Stock Publishers, 2003), 72–73.
[97] Robert L. Reymond (1932-2013), *A New Systematic Theology of the Christian Faith* (Nashville: T. Nelson, 1998), 208.
[98] J. I. Packer (1926-), *Concise Theology: A Guide to Historic Christian Beliefs* (Wheaton, IL: Tyndale House, 1993), 65.

b. The Angel of the Lord, Angel of God
   i) Not every angel is divine, Rev 19:10, 22:9.
   ii) But in many cases the angel is God, Gen 16:6–13, 21:17–20, 22:11–12, 31:11–13, 32:30, 48:15–16, etc.

(John Frame)[99]

The **first** of these principles is nothing else than one fact; here it is: every time in the Holy Bible that we are faced with appearances of this mysterious Angel, whom the Holy Spirit calls *"the Angel of the Face"* (Isa 63:9); *"the Angel of the Covenant"* (Mal 3:1), or *"the Angel of the LORD God"* or *"Angel of Jehovah,"* one understands Him to be attributing constantly all the most incommunicable names of the omnipotent God; and not only the names, but also His attributes and works; and not only His attributes, names and works, but also the worship which everywhere God claims for Himself alone.

… You will understand the Angel of the LORD, who appeared to Jacob in Mesopotamia, saying to this patriarch: 'I am the mighty God of Bethel. I am the LORD, the God of Abraham your father, and the God of Isaac" (Compare Genesis 31:11–13; 28:11–22;

---

[99] John M. Frame (1939-), *The Collected Shorter Theological Writings* (Phillipsburg, NJ: P&R Publishing, 2008).

35:7–15; 48:15, 16, and also 32:24, 28, 30; Hosea 12:4, 5).

(Douglas Kelly)[100]

He is the "angel" who redeems us (Gen. 48:16). He is not a creaturely angel, but the angel of the Lord with whom Jacob wrestled (32:22–32), a pre-incarnate manifestation of the Messiah, according to churchmen throughout history. Centuries after Jacob lived, God came to earth to defeat sin and reveal His faithfulness (John 1:1–18).

(R. C. Sproul)[101]

---

[100] Douglas F. Kelly, *Systematic Theology: Grounded in Holy Scripture and Understood in the Light of the Church*, vol. 1 (Ross-shire, Scotland: Mentor, 2008), 479–480.
[101] R. C. Sproul (1939-2017), *Tabletalk Magazine, November 2007: The English Reformation* (Lake Mary, FL: Ligonier Ministries, 2007), 47.

Excerpts from "Judgments of the Jewish Church"

CHAP. VIII.

That the authors of the apocryphal books acknowledged a Plurality and a Trinity in the Divine nature.

HAVING FINISHED OUR general reflections on the traditional sense of the Scriptures, which was received among the Jews before the time of our Lord Jesus Christ, and of the books wherein we can find such a tradition, it is time for us to come now to the chief matter of our purpose. The question is whether the Jews before Christ's time had any notion of a Trinity, or not? For the Socinians would make us believe, that Justin Martyr, having been formerly a Platonist, and then turning Christian, was the first to invent this doctrine, or rather he adopted it out of the Platonic and into the Christian divinity; and that neither the Jewish nor the Christian Church had ever before conceived any notion of a Trinity or of any plurality in the Divine essence.

The doctrine of the Trinity supposes the Divine essence to be common to three Persons, distinguished from one another by incommunicable properties. These Persons are called by St. John: the Father, the Word, and the Spirit (1Jn 5:7). *"There are three,"* he says, *"that bear witness in heaven, the Father, the Word, and the Spirit; and these three are one."*

This personal distinction supposes the Father is not the Son nor the Holy Ghost, and that the Son is not the Father nor the Holy Spirit. Revelation teaches that the Son is begotten of the Father and that the Holy Spirit proceeds from the Father and the Son, or from the Father by the Son. This distinction is the foundation of their order and of their operations.

For although the unity of the Divine nature makes it necessary that these three Persons should all cooperate in the works of God *ad extra* [external, outward, towards the outside], as we call them, nevertheless there being a certain order among the Persons, and a distinction founded in their personal properties, the Holy Scripture mentions an economy in their operations; so that one work *ad extra* is ascribed to the Father, another to the Son, and a third to the Holy Spirit.

But this distinction of Persons, all partaking of the same common nature and majesty, does not hinder their being equally the object of that worship which religion commands us to pay to God.

I will touch on this matter only very briefly, because my business is only to examine whether the Jews had any notion of this doctrine, or not. Our opinion is this, that though the Gospel has proposed that doctrine more clearly and distinctly, yet there were in the Old Testament sufficient notices of it, so that the Jews before Christ's time did draw from them their notions concerning it.

On the contrary, the Socinians maintain, this doctrine is not only equally foreign to the books of the Old and New Testament, but it was altogether unknown to the Jews before and after Christ, until Justin Martyr first brought it into the Church.

In opposition to this, I affirm the truth as such:

1. That the Jews before Jesus Christ had a notion of a plurality in God, following certain traces of this doctrine that are found in the books of Moses and the Prophets.

2. That the same Jews, following the Scriptures of the Old Testament, acknowledged a Trinity in the Divine nature.

I begin the examination of this subject by considering the notions of the authors of the apocryphal books.[102] One cannot expect that these authors should have explained their mind with relation to the notions of a plurality and of a Trinity in the Godhead as if they had been interpreters of the books of the Old Testament. But they express it sufficiently apart from them, and speak in such a manner that nobody can deny that they must have had those very notions, since it appears that their expressions in speaking of God suppose the notions of a plurality in the Godhead, and of a Trinity in particular. Let us consider some of those expressions.

1. They were so full of the notion of a plurality, which is expressed in Gen 1:26, that the author of

---

[102] What we deem as "Apocrypha" usually consists of the following dozen or so books all in existence at the time of the NT: 1 Esdras (Vulgate 3 Esdras); 2 Esdras (Vulgate 4 Esdras); Tobit; Judith; Rest of Esther (Vulgate Esther 10:4 – 16:24); Wisdom; Ecclesiasticus (also known as Sirach); Baruch and the Epistle of Jeremy ("Jeremiah" in Geneva) (all part of Vulgate Baruch); Song of the Three Children (Vulgate Daniel 3:24–90); Story of Susanna (Vulgate Daniel 13); The Idol Bel and the Dragon (Vulgate Daniel 14); Prayer of Manasseh; 1 Maccabees; 2 Maccabees. There are NT Apocrypha, but these are usually not what people have in mind. There are OT Pseudepigrapha, but the same goes for those. For a brief explanation see Douglas Van Dorn, "Apocrypha," *Decablog* (March 13, 2015), https://thedecablog.wordpress.com/tag/apocrypha/.

Tobit has used it as the form of marriage among the Jews of old, "*Let us make for him a helper.*" So, Tobit 8:6, "*You made Adam, and for him you made his wife Eve as a helper and support. From the two of them the human race has sprung. You said, 'It is not good that the man should be alone; let us make a helper for him like himself;*" whereas in the Hebrew it is only, "*I shall make.*"

Secondly. We see that they acknowledge the creation of the world by the Word of God and by the Holy Ghost, as David. "*By the word of the LORD the heavens were made, and by the Spirit of his mouth all their host*" (Ps 33:6). So the Book of Wisdom 9:1, "*O God of my fathers, and Lord of mercy, who has made all things with your Word,*" or more properly "*by your Word,*" as it is explained in the second verse ("*and by your Wisdom have formed man…*"); and vs. 4. he asks Wisdom in these words, "*Give me Wisdom, that sits by your throne;*" and vs. 17, "*Who has learned your counsel, unless you have given Wisdom and Sent your Holy Spirit from on high?*" where he distinguished the *Logos*, or Wisdom, and the Holy Spirit, from God, to whom he directs his prayer. And so the Book of Judith 16:13-14, "*I will sing to the Lord a new song: O Lord, you are great and glorious, wonderful in strength, and invincible. Let all creatures serve you: for you spoke, and they were made, you sent forth your Spirit, and it created them, and there is none that can resist your voice.*"

Thirdly. They speak of the emanation of the Word from God: those are the words of Wisdom 7:25. "*For she is the breath of the power of God, and a pure influence flowing from the glory of the Almighty: therefore no defiled can thing fall into her.*" That description of Wisdom deserves to be considered, as we have it in the same place (vv. 22-26). For, "*Wisdom, which is the worker of all things, taught me: for in her is a spirit that is intelligent, holy, unique, manifold, subtle, lively, clear, unpolluted, distinct, invulnerable, loving the good, keen, irresistible, beneficent, humane, steadfast, sure, free from anxiety, all-powerful, overseeing all things, and penetrating through all spirits that are intelligent and pure and most subtle. For Wisdom is more mobile than any motion; because of her pureness she pervades and penetrates all things. For she is the breath of the power of God, the brightness of the glory of the Almighty; and the image of his goodness.*" And indeed St. Paul has borrowed from this what we read touching the Son, that he is the brightness of God's glory, and the express image of his person (Heb 1:3). So the Book of Ecclesiasticus says, "*That it is come out of the mouth of the Most High*" (Sirach 24:3).

4thly. There are several names in Scripture which serve to express the second Person: the Son, the Word, the Wisdom, the Angel of the Lord, but who is the Lord indeed. Now those authors use all these names to express a second Person.

For they acknowledge a Father; and a Son, by a natural consequence. Thus the author of Ecclesiasticus, "*I called upon the Lord the Father of my Lord*" (Sir 51:10), in the same way as David speaks of the Messiah (Ps 2 and 110), and as Solomon in his Proverbs (8:25) as of a son in the bosom of his father, and 30:4, "*What is his sons name, if you can tell?*"

They speak of the *Logos* as the Creator of all things; so the author of Wisdom 9:1, "*O God of my fathers, and Lord of mercy, who has made all things with your Word;*" or more properly *by your Word*. And so they call that Wisdom the worker of all things (Wis 7:22).

They speak of the Wisdom in the same words as Solomon does (Prov 3 and 8:22), where he expresses the true notion of eternity. And indeed, they attribute her to have been eternal (Sir 24:18).[103]

They refer constantly to God himself, that is, to the *Logos* of God, as we shall hereafter show at large, what is attributed to the Angel of the Lord in many places of the books of Moses, as to have delivered the Israelites from the Red Sea. So Wisdom 19:9, "*They went at large like horses, and leaped like lambs, praising you, O Lord, who had delivered them.*" Again, to have had his throne in a cloudy pillar (Sir 24:4). To have been caused by the Creator of all things to rest and to have his dwelling in Jacob, and to have his inheritance in

---

[103] Some translations do not have vs. 18. But the LXX reads, "*I am the mother of fair love, and fear, and knowledge, and holy hope: I therefore, being eternal, am given to all my children which are named of him.*"

Israel (8), and so to have given his memorial to his children, which is the law commanded for a heritage into the congregation of Jews (23).

So they attribute to him to have spoken with Moses, "*He made him to hear his voice, and brought him into the dark cloud, and gave him commandments before his face, even the law of life and knowledge, that he might teach Jacob his covenants, and Israel his judgments*" (Sir 45:5).

Again, to have come down from heaven to fight against the Egyptians, "*Your almighty Word leaped down from heaven, out of your royal throne, as a fierce man of war into the midst of a land of destruction.*" And brought your authentic commandment "*as a sharp sword,*" and standing up filled all things with "*death,*" and it touched the heaven, but it stood upon the "*earth*" (Wis 18:15-16).[104]

So they maintain that the angel who appeared to Joshua (Josh 5:13-15) was the Lord himself; so the author of Ecclesiasticus, "*He called upon the most high Lord, when the enemies pressed upon him on every side; and the great Lord heard him. And with hailstones of mighty power he made the battle to fall violently upon the nations, and in the descent [of Bethhoron] he destroyed those who resisted, that the nations might know all their strength, because he fought in the sight of the Lord, and he followed the Mighty One*" (Sir 46:5-6). They refer the miracles wrought by Elijah to the *Logos*, as you see in Ecclesiasticus 48:3,

---

[104] The original adds vs. 17 to the reference.

4, 5). "*By the Word of the Lord he shut up the heavens, and also three times brought down fire. O Elijah, how honored you were in your wondrous deeds! And who has the right to boast which you have? You who raised a corpse from death and from Hades, by the word of the Most High.*"

As there is nothing more common in the Old Testament than to call the *Logos* the Angel of the Lord, because the Father sent him to do all things under the former dispensations, so one can see that there is nothing more ordinary in the apocryphal books, than to speak of an angel in particular, to whom are attributed all the things which could not be performed but by God.

Three things prove clearly that they did not conceive that angel to be a created angel, but an Angel who is God.

First. Because they have this maxim, according to the constant divinity of the Jews, grounded upon Scripture (Deut 32:9) that God took Israel for his portion among all the nations of the world, as if he had left the other nations to the conduct of angels (see Esther 13:15).[105]

---

[105] There are several recensions (revised editions) of Esther 13:15. One English translation it reads, "*And now, O Lord, O king, O God of Abraham, have mercy on your people, because our enemies resolve to destroy us, and extinguish your inheritance. Despise not your portion, which you have redeemed for yourself out of Egypt. Hear my supplication, and be merciful to your lot and inheritance, and turn our mourning into joy, that we may live and praise your name, O Lord, and shut not the mouths of them that sing to you*" (Est 13:15-17).

Second. Because they refer to the *Logos* some histories of the Old Testament, which the Jews till this day refer to an uncreated Angel, or to the Logos, or Shekinah, or Memra of Jehovah, as I shall prove afterwards. We see it in Wisdom 16:12, "*For it was neither herb, nor poultice cured them, but it was your Word, O Lord, that helps all people.*" Also Wisdom 18:15-16, "*Your Almighty Word leaped down from heaven out of your royal throne, as a fierce man of war into the midst of a land of destruction, and brought your authentic commandment as a sharp sword, and standing up filled all things with death; and it touched the heaven, but it stood upon the earth.*" I thought fit to repeat this here, to make Mr. N. ashamed. For he has exposed those ideas and laughed at them, which I believe he would not have done if he had but considered two things. The first is that this Logos who is spoken of is that very man of war mentioned in Moses' song (Ex 15:3)[106] and in Judith (9:7).[107] The other is that St. Paul has followed the notions of the Book of Wisdom, speaking of a sharp sword, which is to be understood, not of the Gospel, but of the Logos (Heb 4:12).[108] But Mr. N. was in the right to ridicule such an authority, which destroys to the ground the

---

[106] "*The Lord is a man of war, the Lord is his name.*"
[107] "*Behold now, the Assyrians are increased in their might; they are exalted, with their horses and riders; they glory in the strength of their foot soldiers; they trust in shield and spear, in bow and sling, and now not that you are the Lord who crushes wars; the Lord is your name.*"
[108] "*The Word of God is living and active, sharper than any tow-edged sword...*"

principles of the Unitarians; for nothing can be more clear, than that this author acknowledges a plurality in God; that the *Logos* must be a Person, and a Person equal to the Father, since he is set upon the royal throne.

Third. Because they bring such appearances of that Angel, it shows they conceived of him as the God who ruled Israel, and who had taken their temple for the place of his abode. And, on the contrary, they speak of God, whom they considered as dwelling in the temple, with the same words which are used in Scripture, when it is spoken of the name of God (Ex 23:31 and 1Sa 8:16[109]), of the angel of the covenant (Mal 3:1), and such expressions. So you see in the first Book of Esdras, "*If any one of you, therefore, is of his people, may his Lord be with him, and let him go up to Jerusalem, which is in Judea, and build the house of the Lord of Israel—he is the Lord who dwells in Jerusalem*" (1Esd 2:5). And again, "*When the young man went out, he lifted up his face to heaven toward Jerusalem, and praised the king of heaven*" (4:58). And Judith 5:18[110] and 9:8.[111] and 2

---

[109] This reference is rather inexplicable. The citation 1Sa 8:16 has nothing to do with the name of God. The closest I find with these numbers is 2Sa 6:18, "*David … blessed the people in the name of the LORD of hosts.*" The context does have to do with the temple as well.
[110] This verse does have to do with the temple, but it does not support the point other than calling it "*the temple of their God.*" I cannot figure out the typo here.
[111] "*Break their strength by your might and bring down their power in your anger; for they intend to defile your sanctuary, and to pollute the

Maccabees 1:25, "*The only giver of all things, the only just, almighty and everlasting, you who delivered Israel from all trouble, and did choose the fathers and sanctify them.*" And 2:17, "*We hope also, that the God that delivered all his people, and has returned the inheritance to all, and the kingship and priesthood, and the sanctuary.*" And 14:35, "*O Lord of all things, who has need of nothing, you were pleased that the temple of your habitation should be among us.*"

I can add, fourthly, that they distinguish exactly the Angel of God from the prophets, though they are called by the same name of angels or messengers, and they distinguish him from angels, whom as creatures they exhort to praise God, as in the Prayer of Azariah, "*O you angels of the Lord, bless ye the Lord, praise and exalt him above all forever*" (PrAz 36 LXX). Such a distinction appears in 1 Esdras 1:50-51, "*Nevertheless the God of their fathers sent by his messenger (aggelos) to call them back, because he spared them and his tabernacle also. But they mocked his messengers (aggelos), and, whenever the Lord spoke, they made a sport of his prophets.*" Also in Tobit 5:16 (LXX), "*So they were well pleased. Then said he to Tobias, 'Prepare your for the journey, and God send you a good journey. And when his son had prepared all things for the journey, his father said, Go with this man, and God, who dwells in heaven, prosper your journey, and the Angel of God keep you company.*" This is just like the prayer of Jacob

---

tabernacle where your glorious name rests, and to cast down the horn of your altar with the sword" (Jdt 9:8).

in Genesis 48:16, "*The Angel who redeemed me from all evil, bless the boys.*" And that very Angel is called God by Jacob in the verse before. Then there is Ecclesiasticus (Sirach) 17:17. "*For in the division of the nations of the whole earth he set a ruler over every people; but Israel is the Lord's portion.*" Also in the Epistle of Jeremiah vv. 6, 7, "*But say in your heart, 'O Lord, we must worship you. For my Angel is with you, and I myself am watching for your souls.*" In the Greek, caring for their souls is referred to the same Angel. Again in 2 Maccabees 11:6, "*When Maccabeus and his men got word that Lysias was besieging the strongholds, they and all the people, with lamentations and tears, prayed to the Lord to send a good Angel to deliver Israel.*"

To show that the Jews before Jesus Christ had such a notion of the *Logos* who was to save his people, we must take notice of two things. First, that the author of the books of Maccabees speaks of God at the end of his book in the same terms which are used by Jacob in Genesis 48:15-16 and are to be referred to the *Logos*, not to a created angel, as I have explained it in a particular discussion of that very place of Genesis.

Second, the Greek interpreters of Scripture have used a method of translating some places of the prophets, which shows they understood that the Messiah should be the very Angel of the Lord who is called the Counsellor, and that the Angel of the Lord was the Lord himself. Two examples will show that clearly.

The first is in that famous oracle of Isaiah 9:6, they have these words, *hoti paidon egennēthē hēmin uios kai edothē hēmin ou hē arxē egenēthē epi tou ōmou outou kai kaletai to onoma outou megalēs boulēs aggelos*. The end (*megalēs boulēs aggelos*) reads, "*The Angel of the great counsel*,"[112] whereas in the Hebrew it is said, he shall be called the "wonderful"[113] (*pele', "wonderful"*) (which is the very word that the Angel of the Lord gives to himself in Judges 13:18) "*the Counsellor of the Mighty God;*" and it is clear that they understood these words to refer to the Messiah, who is spoken of as the son of David (Isa 9:7) in the same words which are used in Psalm 72.

The other example is in this other famous place of Isaiah 63:9 where they have translated, "*... nor an angel, but himself saved them,*" as if they had read *la-'ă'šer* instead of *lō-ṣār*, which we translate as "now." Some of the modern Jews are mightily entangled in explaining that place, but it appears that these interpreters of Isaiah looked upon *the face of God* to have been God

---

[112] This text from the LXX was a vital and very commonly quoted passage by the Church Fathers, used to demonstrate the link between the Angel and Christ. It is usually translated "Angel of the great counsel," but can be translated as "Angel of the great council" (see De Gols in another volume in this series) as in the divine council of the heavenly beings that rule over the affairs of the cosmos (cf. 1Kg 22:19-23, Dan 4:17; 7:9ff., etc.). In citing "wonderful" and the link to the Angel in Judges 13:18 (cf. Gen 32:29; Ex 15:3, 11), Allix is giving one of the reasons why it may have been translated this way.

[113] Allix' original has "admirable," but the way modern translation render it is "wonderful," which is consistent in other related passages (cf. Ex 15:11; Ps 77:14).

himself, which is the reason of their translation, and shows that they understood *the face of the Lord*, which is so often spoken of by Moses, to be the *Logos*, which is *Jehovah*. I can add a reflection concerning their version of the Daniel 3:25. *Species quarti similis filio Dei* ("the fourth is like a/the Son of God"), as Aquila a Jew says,[114] who lived under Hadrian; but the ancient Greeks had translated it *similis Angelo Dei* (like an/the Angel of God)[115] as say an old scholion [notes], related by Drusius (*Fragmentis*, p. 1213), which shows that the ancient Hellenists had the same notion of the Angel of God as of the Son of God. But all those things shall be better understood when we come to the authority of the other Jews, which we will produce later.

Some perhaps may think that the Book of Ecclesiasticus supposes the Wisdom which we maintain to be eternal, to have been created (*ektisthē*), and so says that author (Sir 1:4; 24:9). But I take notice of three things. First. That such an objection may be good in the mouth of an Arian, but not at all in the mouth of a Socinian, and much less in the mouth of an Unitarian of this kingdom, after their writers have owned that the *Logos*, or Word of God, signifies the essential virtue of God.

---

[114] He quotes the Vulgate but refers to the Aquila (fl. 130 A.D.) who translated the OT into Greek and whom Jerome used from liberally in his Latin translation.
[115] The LXX reads "angel of God," while Greek Theodosian reads "Son of God."

Second. The author of Ecclesiasticus follows in that expression the very words of the Greek version of Proverbs 8:22 where it answers to the word possessed, which is not *ektisthē* (create) but *ektēthē*.[116]

Third. That the word *ektisthē*, although we should suppose it to be the true reading, can mean many things; and indeed Aristobulus, a Jew of Alexandria, who lived about the same age of the authors of those apocryphal books (d. 103 B.C.),[117] and whose words are quoted by Eusebius (*Preparation for the Gospel* 1.7.14. p. 324) declares that the Wisdom which Solomon speaks of in the Book of Proverbs was before heaven and earth, and the very author of Ecclesiasticus calls it positively *"eternal"* (Sir 24:18).

There is another objection which is backed by the authority of Grotius, who by the *Logos*, or Wisdom, understands a created angel; but I shall show afterwards the absurdity of that opinion of Grotius; and his error is so plain, that Mr. N. and the Unitarian authors have been ashamed to follow his authority in this point, daring not to maintain that the *Logos* in the first of St. John signified an angel, which they would have done, if they could have digested the absurdity of Grotius's notions upon that place of Wisdom 18:15.

---

[116] His Greek typing here is inexplicable. The LXX actually has *ektisen* (created). Allix clearly has the Hebrew *qanah* ("to possess," "acquire) in mind.

[117] Aristobulus of Alexandria (181-124 B.C.). A Hellenistic Jewish philosopher, was the predecessor of Philo and tried to fuse Hebrew Scriptures with Greek thought.

As for the Holy Ghost, that they acknowledged him for a Person, and for a Divine one, there is as much evidence from the same apocryphal books.

First. I have noted that they attributed to him the creation of the world, as you see in Judith 16:14. "*You sent forth your Spirit, and it created them,*" which is an imitation of David's notions (Psalm 33:6).

Second. They call him the mouth of the Lord. So in the 1 Esdras, "*But Josiah did not turn back his chariot, but tried to fight with him, and did not heed the words of Jeremiah the prophet from the mouth of the Lord*" (1Esd 1:28). "*He also did evil in the sight of the Lord and cared not for the words that were spoken to him by the prophet Jeremy from the mouth of the Lord*" (47; also vs. 57).

Third. They speak of the Bina, or "*understanding,*" by which is to be understood the Holy Spirit, from Proverbs 3 and 8. So in Ecclesiasticus, "*Wisdom has been created before all things, and the understanding of prudence from everlasting*" (Sir 1:4). Also the Book of Wisdom, "*Because wisdom will not enter a deceitful soul, nor dwell in a body enslaved to sin. For the Holy Spirit of discipline will flee from deceit, and will rise and depart from foolish thoughts, and will be ashamed at the approach of unrighteousness. For Wisdom is a loving spirit, and will not acquit a blasphemer of his words; because God is witness of his inmost feelings, and a true observer of his heart, and a hearer of his tongue. Because the Spirit of the Lord has filled the* world, and that which holds all things together has knowledge of the voice" (Wis 1:4-7).

Fourth. They acknowledge him to be the Counsellor of God who knew all his counsels. So you read in the Book of Wisdom, "*Who has learned your counsel, unless you have given Wisdom and sent your Holy Spirit from above?*" (Wis 9:17).

Fifth. They speak of him as of him who discovers the secrets of God, "*He will reveal instruction in his teaching, and will glory in the law of the Lord's covenant*" (Sir 39:8). And again, "*By the spirit of might he saw the last things and comforted those who mourned in Zion. He revealed what was to occur to the end of time, and the hidden things before they came to pass*" (Sir 48:24).

Sixth. They acknowledge him to be sent from God, "*Who has learned your counsel, unless you have given wisdom and sent your Holy Spirit from on high?*" (Wis 9:17).

After all, if we consider what notions they had of the Messiah who was promised to them, we will find that they had much nobler ideas than those which are now entertained by the latter Jews, and more like to them which we find among the Prophets.

First. It is clear that they looked upon him as the Person who was to sit upon the throne of God; the title of my Lord which is given by the author of Ecclesiasticus (51:10) shows beyond exception by a clear allusion to the Psalm 110:1 which speak both of the Messiah.[118]

Second. They did not look upon it as an absurd thing to suppose that God is to appear in the earth, as you see in Baruch 3:37. *"Afterward he appeared upon the earth and lived among men."* Here it refers either to his appearance upon Sinai or to the incarnation of the *Logos*.

Third. They suppose another coming of the Messiah, and then *"the saints are to judge the nations, and have dominion over the people, and their Lord shall reign forever"* (Wisdom 3:8). These words have been borrowed by St. Paul (1Co 6:2).[119]

Fourth. They acknowledge such appearances of God, as we have an example in 2 Maccabees 11:6, *"When Maccabeus and his men got word that Lysias was besieging the strongholds, they and all the people, with lamentations and tears, prayed to the Lord to send a good Angel to deliver Israel"* (cf. 15:22-23).[120]

---

[118] "*I appealed to the Lord, the Father of my Lord, not to forsake me in the days of affliction, at the time when there is no help against the proud*" (Sir 51:10). Psalm 110:1, "*The LORD [Yahweh] said to my Lord [Adonai]: 'Sit at my right hand, until I make your enemies your footstool.'*" This verse is used many times by the NT to prove that Jesus is the Son of the Father.

[119] "*Do you not know that the saints will judge the world?*"

[120] "*And he called upon him in these words: 'O Lord, you sent your angel in the time of Hezekiah king of Judea, and he slew fully a hundred and eighty-five thousand in the camp of Sennacherib. So now, O Sovereign of the heavens, send a good angel to carry terror and trembling before us.*"

Fifth. They speak of the appearances of God as an *epiphaneia*, which is the very word used by St. Paul for the first and second "appearance" of Jesus Christ. "*So every man praised toward the heaven the glorious Lord, saying, 'Blessed be he that hath kept his own place undefiled. So that fighting with their hands, and praying to God with their hearts, they slew no less than thirty and five thousand men; for through the appearance of God they were greatly cheered*" (2Ma 15:34, 27).

Sixth. They expected at the second coming of the Messiah such a manifestation of his glory as in the consecration of the temple. "*And then the Lord will disclose these things, and the glory of the lord and the cloud will appear, as they were shown in the case of Moses, as Solomon asked that the place should be specially consecrated*" (2Ma 2:8).

I believe these proofs are sufficient to demonstrate, 1. That there was before Jesus Christ's time a notion of plurality in the Godhead. 2. That they believed that such a plurality was a Trinity. 3. That they looked upon the Son or the Logos and the Holy Ghost not as created beings, but as beings of the same Divine Nature with the Father, by an eternal emanation from him, as having the same power and the same majesty.

But these ideas of the apocryphal books will appear clearer when we take them in conjunction with the explication of the same notions among other Hebrew writers, which I shall now consider more particularly, and in addition to those places of Scripture on which they ground their explications.

CHAP. XII.

That the Jews had a distinct notion of the Word as of a Person and of a Divine Person at that.

THE GREAT PART OF THE DISPUTE we have with the Socinians depends on the true meaning of the first chapter of St. John's Gospel, where the *Logos* is spoken of as having created the world, was in time made flesh, and whom we Christians look upon as the promised Messiah. I do not think I can do the truth a greater service than by clarifying this notion of the *Logos* and showing what thoughts the ancient Jews had concerning it.

Socinus confesses that the *Logos* is a Person; for he owns that St. John did describe the man Christ Jesus by the *Logos* and attributed to him the creation of the Church, which is, according to him, the new world. But here in England, the followers of Socinus will not stand by this exposition but understand by the *Logos* that virtue by which God created heaven and earth, as Moses relates in Genesis 1. They obstinately deny this virtue to be a person, i. e. an intelligent subsistence, and rather look upon it as a Divine attribute, which, they say, was particularly discovered in the mission of Jesus Christ for the salvation of mankind.

It cannot be denied by them that St. John, being one of the circumcision, wrote with a special respect to the Jews, so that they might understand him, and receive benefit by it; and therefore it cannot be doubted, but that when he called Jesus Christ the *Logos*, he used a word that was commonly known among the Jews of those times in which he lived.

Otherwise, if he had used this word in a sense not commonly known to the Jews, he would have signified to them the new idea he alone had fastened to it. But he gives not the least intimation of anything new in it, though he uses the word so many times in the very beginning of his Gospel. It is certain therefore, that he used it in the sense that it was then commonly understood by the Jews.

Now the idea the Jews had of the *Logos* was the same they had of a real and proper person, that is, a living, intelligent, free principle of action. That this was their notion of the *Logos*, or Word, we shall prove by the works of Philo and the Chaldee paraphrases [i.e. the Targums].

I'll begin with Philo. He conceives the Word to be a true and proper cause: for he declares, in about a hundred places, that God created the world by his Word. He conceived the Word to be an intelligent cause; because in him, according to Philo, are the original ideas of all things that are expressed in the works of the creation.[121]

He makes the Word a cooperator with God in the creation of man, and says that God spoke those words to him, "*Let us make man*" (Gen 1:26). It may be added that he calls the Word "the image of God," and makes man the image of this image.[122]

These are some of the characters that represent the Word as a true Person. But there are others no less demonstrative of this truth. 1. Philo asserts that the *Logos* is begotten of God (*Allegorical Interpretation* 2) which can agree only to a person. 2. He proves that the Word acted and spoke in all the Divine appearances that are mentioned in the Old Testament; which certainly supposes a person. 3. He describes the Word as presiding over the empires of the world and determining the changes that befall them.[123] Where he brings in the Word for a mediator between God and men[124] that renders God propitious to his creatures,[125] that is, the instructor of men[126] and their shepherd, alluding to Psalm 23:1.[127]

The Chaldee paraphrases are full of notions and expressions relating to the Word, conformable to

---

[121] Philo, *On the Creation of the World* 8-9.
[122] Philo, *Who Is the Heir of Divine Things* 231.
[123] Philo, *That God is Unchangeable* 176.
[124] Philo, *Who Is the Heir of Divine Things* 205-206.
[125] Philo, *On Dreams* 1.66.
[126] Ibid. 1.68.
[127] Philo, *On the Change of Names* 115-116.

those of Philo when he discusses the *Logos*, so that he must wink hard who does not see that in their sense the Word is truly a Person. We see this in the following ways:

1. They almost always distinguish the Memra, or Word of the Lord, which is the Aramaic equivalent to Philo's Greek *Logos*, from the word *Pithgama*, which signifies a matter or a discourse, as does in Greek.
2. They ascribe the creation of the world to the Word.
3. They make it the Word who appeared to the ancients under the name of the Angel of the Lord.
4. They have the Word who saved Noah in the time of the Flood and made a covenant with him (Onkelos on Gen 6:7, 8:21).
5. They say that Abraham believed in the Word, which thing was imputed to him for righteousness (Onk. on Gen 15:6).
6. They say that the Word brought Abraham out of Chaldea, (Onk. on Gen 15:7) and commanded him to sacrifice (Gen 15:9) and gave him the prophecy related vs. 13.
7. They have Abraham swearing by the Word (Onk. on Gen 21:23).
8. For them the Word succored Ishmael (Gen 21:20) and Joseph in his bondage (Gen 39:2-3).

Targum Onkelos continues these translations in his Targum on Exodus:

1. It is the Word's assistance that God promises to Moses (Ex 3:12; 4:12; 18:19)
2. It is the Word in whom Israel believed, as well as in Moses (Ex 14:32).
3. It is the Word who redeems Israel out of Egypt (Ex 15:2).
4. It is the Word against whom Israel murmured in Sin (Ex 16:8).
5. It is the Word before whom the people marched to receive the Law (Ex 19:17).
6. It is the Word whose presence is promised in the tabernacle (Ex 29:42; 30:6 which is repeated in vs. 36).[128]
7. It is between the Word and Israel the sabbath is made a sign (Ex 31:13, 17).[129]
8. It is the Word whose protection was promised Moses, when he desired to see God (Ex 33:22-23).

Onkelos has the same things on Leviticus and Numbers.

1. It is the Word whose commandments the Israelites were to carefully observe (Lev 8:35; 18:30; 22:9; Num 9:19; 20:24).

---

[128] Num 8:29 is an inexplicable typo. This passage does not have the Word in it, nor is he talking about Numbers until the next section. Ex 30:36 does repeat vs. 6 and is in the same chapter.
[129] The original reads, "...and so also Lev 36:46. This is an inexplicable typo to which I can find no resolution.

2. It is spoken of the Word, that he will not forsake the people, if they continue in their obedience (Lev 26:11).[130]
3. By the Word God looks upon his people (Ibid).
4. The majesty of the Word rested among the Israelites (Num 11:20).
5. It is the Word whom Moses exhorts the Jews not to rebel against (Num 14:9; 20:24).
6. They believed in the Word (Num 14:11; 20:12).
7. The Word meets Balaam (Num 23) and opens his eyes (22:31).

Yet again, the same things, or the like, we find in Onkelos on Deuteronomy:

1. The Word brought Israel out of Egypt and fought for them (Dt 1:30; 3:22; 8:2-3; 20:1).
2. The Word led Israel in the pillar of a cloud (1:32-33; cf. 33:3).[131]
3. The Word spoke out of the fire at Horeb (4:33, 36). Moses was mediator between the Word and his people (5:5).
4. Moses exhorts the Jews to obey the Word (13:19; 15:5; 26:14; 28:1, 2, 15, 45, 62; 30:8, 10, 20).
5. The Word conducts Israel under Joshua to the land of Canaan (31:6, 8).
6. The Word created the world (33:27).

---

[130] The original 28:11 should probably be 26:11.
[131] The original reads only 1:32. The "cloud" verse is in the next verse. I have added 33:3 where they are both in the same verse.

You can see how agreeable the notions of Onkelos are with those of Philo, even though the one wrote in Egypt and the other in Palestine, and both before the time of our Lord Jesus Christ.

But besides Onkelos on the Pentateuch, we have two other paraphrases: the one, which is very diffuse,[132] is said to be Targum Jonathan's; the other, which is called the Jerusalem Targum,[133] and is short, and, as it seems, imperfect. The reader may soon judge by comparing them, whether they differ from Philo and Onkelos, or not:

1. The Jerusalem Targum says that God created the world by his Wisdom, which he grounds on the word *Bereshith* (Gen 1:1). And Philo means the same thing, when he calls the *Logos*, *arche* (the first emanation or firstborn word; *The Confusion of Languages* 146).
2. The same Targum says, the Word made man after his image (Gen 1:27).
3. Jonathan's affirms that the garden of Eden was planted by the Word for the just before the creation of the world (Gen 2:8).
4. Both Jonathan's and the Jerusalem Targum say the Word spoke to Adam in the garden (Gen 3:8-10); and that the Word lifted up Enoch to heaven (Gen 5:24).

---

[132] Perhaps he means here more than one author.
[133] Sometimes equated with Targum Neofiti.

5. Jonathan's affirms that the Word protected Noah and shut the door of the ark upon him (Gen 7:16).
6. That the Word threw down the tower at Babel (Gen 11:8).
7. Both have it that God promised Abraham that his Word should protect him (Gen 15:1).
8. Jonathan's makes it the Word who plagued Pharaoh for Abraham's sake (Gen 12:17).
9. The Jerusalem Targum says it was the Word who appeared to Abraham at the tent door (Gen 18:2); and that the Word rained fire from before the Lord (Gen 19:24).
10. Both this Targum and Jonathan's say that Abraham taught his people to hope in the name of the Word of the Lord (Gen 21:33).
11. The Jerusalem Targum makes Abraham say, The Word of the Lord will prepare a sacrifice (Gen 22:8); and asserts that Abraham invoked the Word and called him Lord in his prayer (Gen 22:14).
12. Jonathan's Targum brings in Abraham swearing by the Word of the Lord (Gen 24:3); and God promising that his Word would succor Isaac (Gen 26:24, 28 repeated in Gen 31:3).[134]
13. The same Targum says that the Word of the Lord made Rachel bear a child (Gen 30:22); which is in agreement with what Philo says, that the *Logos* caused Isaac to be born (*Alleg.* 1. 2. p. 77).

---

[134] Ch. 23 is a typo. 31:5, 42 and 32:9 are inexplicable, so I have deleted them.

14. According to this Targum, the Word sent Michael to save Tamar (Gen 38:25). The Word went down with Jacob into Egypt (Gen 46:4).
15. The Word succors Joseph (Gen 49:25); which Joseph acknowledges (Gen 50:20).

We may trace the same notions in their Targums on Exodus:

1. According to Jonathan's, the Word built houses for the midwives that feared God (Ex 1:21).
2. The Word caused that miraculous heat which disposed Pharaoh's daughter to go and bathe herself in the Nile (Ex 2:5).
3. It was he who spoke and the world was made, according to Jonathan's Targum; or it was the Word of the Lord, according to the Jerusalem Targum, that spoke to Moses (Ex 3), which clearly shows that they made use of the word Memra to express what is so often repeated, "*And God said*" (Gen 1).
4. It is the Word who, as God promised to Moses, was to be his mouth (Ex 4:12, 15).
5. According to the Jerusalem Targum, the Word appeared to Abraham by the name of the God of heaven; and the name of his Word was not declared to the patriarchs (Ex 6:8).
6. The Word of the Lord slew the first-born of Egypt, (Ex 12:29).
7. The Word of the Lord has appeared on three remarkable occasions: first, at the creation of the world; second, to Abraham; third, at Israel's departure out of

Egypt. A fourth time he shall appear at the coming of the Messiah (thus Jonathan and Targ. Jerusalem on Ex 12:42).

8. The Word wrought miracles by Moses (Ex 13:8).
9. The Word raised up those Israelites which were killed by the Philistines that left Egypt three years before the departure of their brethren out of Egypt (Ex 13:17).
10. For the neglect of the commands of the Word were the Israelites killed (Ex 13:17).
11. It is the Word who looked on the host of the Egyptians; and to him the Israelites cried (Ex 14:24, 31).
12. It is the Word who gives the law concerning the sabbath (Ex 15:25), and he against whom Israel murmured (vs. 8).
13. The Israelites hear the voice of the Word (Ex 19:5), who speaks (vs. 9), and pronounces the Law (20:1); being the same that redeemed Israel from Egypt (*ibid.* and Lev 1).
14. God promises to send his Word with his people, and Israel is strictly enjoined to obey him (Ex 23:20-22).
15. The Word punishes Israel for the golden calf (Ex 33:35).
16. The Word talks with Moses in the tabernacle, and the people worship him (Ex 33:9, 11; Lev 1).
17. It is the Word whose appearance is promised to Moses (Ex 33:19), and the Word is distinguished from the angels that attend him (Ex 33:23).
18. It is the Word to whom Moses prays, and who is called the name of the Lord (Ex 34:5).

These things continue in their Targums on Leviticus, Numbers, and Deuteronomy:

1. The Word makes statutes (Lev 23:11; Num 22:18) according to the same Jonathan.
2. It is the Word of whom the Jerusalem Targum understands what is spoken by Jonathan of the face of the Lord (Num 9:8).
3. By the order of the Word of the Lord the Israelites encamp (Num 9:19, 23).
4. It is the Word to whom prayer is made upon removing the ark of the covenant (Num 10:35, 36).
5. The Word spoke to all the Prophets before Moses (Num 12:6).
6. The Word gives answer (Num 14:20).
7. The Word sent fiery serpents, and those that were healed were healed by the name of the Word of the Lord (Num 21:6, 8, 9).
8. It is before the Word that the idolatrous Israelites were hanged (Num 25:4).
9. It is the Word who wrought wonders in the desert on behalf of Israel (Dt 1:1; 4:34; 6:22) and whom the Israelites provoked (Dt 1:1).
10. The Word multiplied Israel, and fought for them, yet they did not believe in him (Dt 1:10, 30, 32 and 3:2) both in Jonathan and the Jerusalem Targum.
11. The Word punished Israel for the business of Peor (Dt 4:3).
12. The Word sits on a throne high lifted up, and hears the people's prayers, and speaks from the midst of the

fire, and gives the Law (Dt 4:7, 12, 33; vv. 23, 24, 25).
13. Moses is a mediator between the Word and the people (Dt 5).
14. It is by the name of the Word that Israel ought to swear (Dt 6:13).
15. The Word was to drive out the nations before Israel (Dt 11:23).
16. The Word chose the Levites for his service (Dt 21:5) and the whole people of Israel (Dt 26:18).
17. The Word protected Jacob from Laban (Dt 26:5).
18. The Word destroyed Sodom (Dt 29:22).
19. The Word swore to the Patriarchs (Dt 31:7).
20. The Word shall judge the people (Dt 32:36).
21. The Word says of himself, that he was, is, and is to come (Dt 32:39; cf. Rev 1:17-18).
22. The Word takes Moses up to Mount Ibraee (the mountain of Nebo); and Moses prays to him for a sight of the land of Canaan (Dt 32:49).
23. The Word shows Moses the generations of the great men of Israel (Dt 34:1).
24. The Word said he had sworn to give Israel the land of Canaan (Dt 34:4).
25. To conclude, Moses dies according to the decree of the Word of the Lord; that is to say, the Word recalls his soul with a kiss, and with a huge train of angels inters his body; being the same Word who had appeared to him, and sent him into Egypt; and by so many miracles redeemed Israel from there (Dt 34:5, 6, 10, 11, 12).

There is no need of making any profound consideration on these many places of Philo and the Chaldee paraphrases, to convince the reader that the Jews before Jesus Christ did look upon the Word as a true and real Person. The consequence is easily drawn by whomever looks them over with but half an eye.

I know the word *Memra* in the Hebrew is sometimes taken in another sense, as well as that of *Logos* is in the Greek. But all the personal characteristics of action, of commanding, of speaking, of answering, of giving laws, of issuing out decrees, of being prayed to, of receiving worship, and the like, are so expressly given to that Word we now discuss as to render it absurd to take it for anything other than a Person.

Let us next inquire into the nature of this Person, according to the same testimonies of the ancient Jews, whether it be angelic or divine, and consequently whether this Person be truly God.

I propose this, not that I think there is any necessity of proving it after all that I have already observed from the ancient Jews touching the Word; but for the clearer manifestation of the absurdity into which our adversaries fall by their striving to force another sense upon the word, as the more knowing men among them cannot but see, when they consider these proofs with attention.

He who wrote against Vechnerus[135] endeavors in general to persuade us that in those places of the Targums where the *Memra* is spoken of, it is used to express the Divine providence over the faithful of ancient times; or else in particular it signifies the attributes of God, his affections or actions, his miracles, his appearances, his inspirations, and the like. This he repeats in several parts of his dissertation, and at the end of his work he tries to apply it to several texts in the Targum.

One might reasonably doubt whether he himself were satisfied with his own performance in this. I have two great reasons to think he was not. The first is that it seems he never consulted Philo's notions of the *Logos* before he made this judgment, notwithstanding that he could not help but see them in Grotius on St. John's Gospel, which he quotes; and he could not but know how much they were insisted upon by those writers whom he pretended to answer. They do indeed so distinctly and clearly establish the personality of the *Logos* that they render useless and unsuitable all the interpretations he has found out for the texts in the Targums.

The second is that he himself, though he fitted his interpretations to divers passages in the Targum, thereby to break the force of them when turned against him, is yet forced to acknowledge that

---

[135] Probably Daniel Vechner (1572-1632).

sometimes the word *Memra* signifies a person properly so called, according to our use of it. The several places where the Word is said to create the world give him much trouble, though he tries to elude them. And though he endeavors to rid his hands of them by asserting that the Word does there signify the power of God; nevertheless he lets you understand that if you are not pleased with that solution, you may have his consent to take it in the Arian sense of the word, for a created God by whom, as by a real and instrumental cause, God did truly create the universe.

This is the strangest answer that could be returned to so great an objection. For he must have lost his reason who imagines that God can make a creature capable of creating the universe. Grant this and by what character will you distinguish the creature from the Creator? By what right then could God appropriate, as he does very often in the Old Testament, the work of the world's creation to himself, excluding any other from having to do in it but himself? Why should God upon this result forbid the giving of worship to the creature which is due to the Creator? The Arians, who worship Jesus Christ, though they esteem him a creature, and those Papists who swallow whole the doctrine of transubstantiation; they may teach in their schools that a creature may be enabled by God to become a Creator. But as for us, who deny that anything but God is to be adored, as Philo denied it before us (*On the Decalogue* p. 581; *de Monarch*,[136] p. 628), we reject all such vain conceits of a creature being in any way capable of receiving the infinite power of a Creator.

There are other places which he also found he could not easily evade, so that at length he consents that the *Memra* does in fact quite often denote a person in the language of the Targums; such as where we read the Word spoke and the Word said. But what kind of person? An angel, a created angel in his judgment, who speaks in the name of God. And thus, he thinks the Word is to be understood in those paraphrases when they ascribe to the Word the leading of Israel through the desert.

The reader may judge how many texts this answer will fit, by reviewing what has been said in the two foregoing chapters. He will find I have there prevented this answer, and showed that Philo and the Targums did not take this for a created angel, but for a Divine Person, who was called an angel in respect of the office he discharged according to the economy between the three Persons of the blessed Trinity; and of whom the Targums generally make express mention in places where the Hebrew text has *Jehovah Elohim*, or the Angel of the Lord; and sometimes where it has simply the name Jehovah.

---

[136] This work is not listed in the *SBL Handbook of Style* on Philo of Alexandria.

However, to leave no doubt in this matter, we will undertake to prove further that the Word does not signify a created angel in Philo or in the Targums, but a Person truly Divine.

It is true, that Philo sometimes calls the angels *Logos* in the plural. But elsewhere he speaks of the *Logos* singularly, in terms that express his acknowledgment of him for the Creator of angels, and consequently for God. This he does in his book *On the Sacrifices of Cain* (p. 202)[137] where he declares him to be the Word who appeared to Moses, and separates him from the angels, who are the hosts of God.

Again, he describes the *Logos* under the name of *Epistēmē* as true God, as Creator of the world (*Lib. de Temulentia*,[138] p. 190. D. 194. B); but the angels after another manner (*On Planting*, p. 168. F. G.; *On Giants* p. 221. E; *De Mundo*, p. 391).

It is true, he calls the Word an archangel (*On the Confusion of Tongues* 146), but in the same place he calls him the firstborn of God, the image of God, the Creator of the world; and in another place, the Son of God that conducted Israel through the wilderness (*On Husbandry* 51; *The Heir of All Things* 201-205).

He was so far from taking the Word to be an angel that he affirmed the Word used to appear to men under the form of an angel. Thus, he says, the Word

---

[137] Allix possibly has Philo, *Sacrifices* 8 in mind.
[138] This work is not listed in the *SBL Handbook of Style* on Philo of Alexandria.

appeared to Jacob (*On Dreams* 1.189-90); and to Hagar (*On Dreams* 1.238-41). We are to observe this carefully, that we may make Philo agree with Philo: for on one hand he says an angel appeared to the patriarchs; and on the other he says the *Logos* appeared to them. His purpose is to acquaint us with the notion that the *Logos* is named an angel because he appeared as an angel in these kinds of manifestations of himself.

Now as to the Targums, they likewise understand by this Angel a Person that is truly God. For:

1. Could they ascribe the creation of the world to the Word, as they do, and yet think him to be a creature? Could they profess him to be the Creator of mankind, without asserting his Divinity? Could they think him to be no better than an angel, and yet suppose him to be worshipped by men, whom they know to be little lower than the angels? Could they imagine him to have given the Law on mount Sinai, and not make some considerations upon the preface of the Law; wherein the great Lawgiver says, "*I am Jehovah your God, who brought you out of the land of Egypt?*" The Word is not so often called an angel in the Targums, as he is set forth with these characters of God; as the reader may see especially in Jonathan's Targum, and in that of Jerusalem (Ex 3:14; 12:42) and in many other places.
2. The Targums always distinguish the Word from the angels; representing them as messengers employed by the Word, as the Word himself is often described

as God's messenger. Thus, the Targum on 1Kg 19:11, 12;[139] Ps 68:11, 18[140]; 2Chr 32:21.[141]
3. They say the Word was attended with angels, when he gave the Law (Targ. on 1Ch 29:11),[142] and when he assisted at the interment of Moses (Jonathan on Dt 34:6).[143]

---

[139] *"And he said: 'Go forth and stand on the mountain before the Lord.' And behold the Lord was revealing himself, and before him were armies of the angels of the wind breaking apart the mountains and shattering the rocks before the Lord; not in the army of the angels of the wind was the Shekinah of the Lord. And after the army of the angels of the wind was the army of the angels of the earthquake; not in the army of the angels of earthquake was the Shekinah of the Lord. And after the army of the angels of the earthquake was the army of the angels of fire; not in the army of the angels of the fire was the Shekinah of the Lord; and after the army of the angels of the fire was the voice of those who were praising softly.*
[140] *"You set your revival in it, you established the hosts of angels to do good to the poor, O God ... The chariots of God are twice ten thousand of blazing fire; two thousand angels lead them; the Shekinah of the* LORD *dwells among them on Mount Sinai in the sanctuary."*
[141] *"Then the Memra of the Lord sent the angel Gabriel, and during the night of the Passover he destroyed with a molten stream of fire and burnt up their breath within them."*
[142] *"Yours, O Lord, is the greatness, for with great power you created the world, and the might, for you brought our fathers out of Egypt with many mighty acts and brought them across the sea, and you were revealed in splendor upon the mountain of Sinai, with bands of angels, to give the law to your people. You gave victories over Amalek, Sihon, Og and the kings of the Canaanites; in the majesty of your glory you caused the sun to stand still in Gibeon and the moon in the plain of Ajalon, until your people, the house of Israel, were avenged on those who hated them. For all these things are the works of your hand, in heaven and on earth, and you have authority over them and sustain everything which is in heaven and everything which is on earth. Yours, O Lord, is the dominion in the firmament, and you are exalted above all the angels that are in heaven and above all those who are appointed as leaders on earth."*
[143] The text reads in part, *"...for He revealed Himself in His Word, and with Him the companies of ministering angels..."*

4. The Targums represent the Word as sitting on a high throne and hearing the prayers of the people (Jonathan on Dt 4:7).
5. Jonathan says expressly that the Word who spoke to Moses was the same who spoke and the world was made and who was the God of Abraham (Ex 3:14, 15; 6:4). So then if he who was the God of Abraham was only an angel that impersonated God, then he who created the world was a created angel; which, as I have showed, is absurd.
6. It is impossible to explain otherwise what the Jews so unanimously affirm, that God revealed himself face to face to Moses; which is more than he granted any prophet, unless the Word who appeared to Moses was the true God and not a mere angel (see Onk. on Dt 34:10, 11 and the other Targums).

But what, say they, may not an angel bear the name of God, when he represents the Person of God? Was not the ark called *Jehovah,* because it was a symbol of his Person?

Does not Jonathan on Num 11:35, 36 say to the ark, *Revelare Sermo Domini et redi?*[144] This is indeed a

---

[144] "*And it was when the ark should go forward, the Cloud gathered itself together and stood still, not going on, until Mosheh [Moses], standing in prayer, prayed and supplicated mercy from before the Lord, and thus spoke: Let the Word of the Lord be now revealed in the power of Your anger, that the adversaries of Your people may be scattered; and let not the banner of those who hate them be uplifted before You. But when the ark should rest, the Cloud gathered itself to ether and stood, but did not overspread, until Mosheh, standing in prayer, prayed and besought mercy from before the Lord, thus speaking: Return now, Oh Word of the Lord, in the goodness of Your mercy, and lead Your people Israel, and let the glory of Your*

notion which the Socinians have borrowed of Abenezra[145] on Exodus 3 and Joseph (*Albo de Fund*, c. 8). And so they pretend that the pillar of cloud is called the Lord (Ex 13:21, 14:19), that the ark is called the Lord (Num 10:35), that the angel is called the Lord (Jdg 6:15), the name being given to the symbol, viz. the ark; and to the second cause, namely, the angel; because of their representing God.

But to the great displeasure of our modern Jews and Socinians who have borrowed from them their weapons, we have still enough of the ancient Jewish texts left, to show how their sentiments in these matters are quite to contrary.

For, 1. they (as has been already observed) believed that the Angel spoken of in Judges 6:15 was the Word and that this Word created the world, as has been largely proved.

2. The ancients held just the reverse of what our moderns say, as we gather from Philo. For instead of an angel's taking the place of God, he says the *Logos* took the place of an angel (*On Dreams* 1.238-39).

As to the ark, it is folly to imagine that because God promised to dwell and to hear prayers there, and enjoined worship toward it, therefore the ark was

---

Shekinah dwell among them, and (Your) mercy with the myriads of the house of Jakob, and with the multitudes of the thousands of Israel" (Num 10:35-36 PJE).

[145] Abraham ben Meir Ibn Ezra (1089-1167). One of the most distinguished Jewish biblical commentators and philosophers of the Middle Ages.

called Jehovah. The ancient Jews spoke not to the ark, but to God, who resided between the cherubim. This is plainly expressed in those words of Jonathan (Num 10:35-36, *"Let the Word of the Lord be now revealed"* etc.), where the words are not addressed to the ark itself but to him who promised to give them some tokens of his presence, namely, to the Word, who created the world, who redeemed Israel from Egypt, who heard their prayers from over the ark, and who had shut up therein the tables of the Law, which he had given them on mount Sinai.

And thus the Targum on 1Ch 13:6. *"David and all Israel went up to remove the ark of the Lord, who dwells between the cherubim, whose name is called on it;"* or as 2Sam 6:2, *"Whose name is called by the name of the Lord of hosts, who dwells between the cherubim."* In short, the Scripture never gives to any place or creature the name *Jehovah* in the nominative case, either singly or joined with any other noun in apposition. But either in an oblique case, such as *aron YHWH* or with a verb substantive understood, as *Jehovah Nissi, Jehovah Shamma*. Other things that the Socinians have to say against this the reader may see fully answered by Buxtorf in his *Exercitationes ad Historiam*, ch. 1 on the History of the Ark, where the reader shall have a full satisfaction by reading those chapters.

It remains therefore certain that the Word mentioned in Philo and the paraphrases is not an angel but a Divine Person; *Theos* (God) as Philo calls him many times; and if the expression is allowable, *deutros theos* (Second God), as he speaks in Eusebius, *Preparation for the Gospel* 7.13.

But we must now go on to that which will remove all difficulties from this subject and convince the reader, if anything can do it, that the Jews looked upon the *Logos* as a Divine Person. I speak of the appearances of an angel who is called God and worshipped as God under the Old Testament; and I thought it fitting for this very reason to write more upon this subject in order to prevent the objections of the modern Jews and of the Unitarians all at once.

CHAP. XIII.

That all the appearances of God, or of the Angel of the Lord, which are spoken of in the books of Moses, have been referred to the Word by the Jews before Christ's incarnation.

SOME OF THE LATE Jewish commentators that have had disputes with the Christians, particularly those whose comments are collected in the Hebrew Bible printed by Bomberg[146] at Venice, oppose this proposition with all their might. They have laid it down for a rule that wherever God is *said to be present, there all the celestial family is with him*; i.e. the angels, by whose ministry (as they say) God has ordinarily acted in his appearances to men. So Rabbi Solomon Jarchi says on Gen 19:24. Opposed to this were those ancient Jews who followed the tradition of their forefathers. They were not biased by the spirit of dispute with Christians. Rather, they understood the *Chokhmah* (Wisdom) and *Binu* (Understanding) to be Wisdom and the Holy Ghost; as we were admonished

---

[146] Daniel Bomberg (d. 1549). A Christian who printed many important Hebrew books.

by R. Joseph de Karnitol[147] (*Saare Tsedec*, fol. 25. col. 4. and fol 26. col. 2.).

This collection of late commentators are of great use for interpreting the Scriptures. Nevertheless, several divines that have applied themselves to the study of the comments of these Rabbis have been led by them rashly into their same opinion. The renowned Grotius fell into this snare and has had but too many followers. We have no cause to wonder that the Papists do the same, being concerned as they are to find examples in the Old Testament of religious worship paid to angels, the better to cover their idolatry.

But in truth, the modern Jews absolutely depart from the ancient sentiments of their own fathers; and they who follow the modern Jews in this weaken (for lack of due consideration only, I hope) the proofs of the Divinity of Jesus Christ. They do this by yielding to the modern Jews, as an agreed point between them and the Christians, that which is quite contrary to what the Apostles and primitive Christians supposed in their disputes with the Jews of their times, and which our later Jews themselves would never have submitted to if they had known any other way to avoid the arguments that were brought against them out of their own Scriptures.

---

[147] Karnitol is a corruption of Gikatilla. This is R. Joseph b. Abraham Gikatilla.

It behooves us therefore to give just force to those arguments that were used by the Apostles and the Fathers and to restore to the truth all her advantages, by showing how bad of guides our modern Jews are in the matters now before us; and how they have deviated from the constant doctrine of their ancestors in order to find out ways to defend themselves against the Christians.

I affirm then for certain that the appearances of God, or of any Angel who is called Jehovah, or the God of Israel, who is worshipped and spoken of in the Old Testament, were never said by the ancient Jews to refer to created angels who impersonated God. Further, I vouch, that generally the ancient Jews referred these appearances as the Word, whom they distinguished from angels, as they do God from the creature. This thereby justified the patriarchs in paying divine worship and adoration to him that appeared to them, according to these ancient Jews.

To prove this, I must return to Philo's opinion which I have had occasion to speak about in several places. I would willingly spare myself the trouble, and my reader the nauseousness of repeating the same things; but this is a matter of such importance as necessarily obliges me, by a particular enumeration of passages, to produce Philo's judgment on this point, as I have done already. He is indeed so ample, and so much ours in his testimony concerning the dignity of the Angel that appeared to the Fathers, that he could not say more if we had hired him to give evidence on our side:

1. In general, he asserts, that it was the Word who appeared to Adam, Jacob, and Moses; though in the books of Moses it is only an angel that is spoken of [*On Dreams* 189, 192, 194].
2. It was the Word who appeared to Abraham (Gen 18:1) according to Philo; for he says, it was the Word who promised Sarah a son in her old age, and that enabled her to conceive and bring forth [*Allegorical Interpretation III.217*].
3. It was the Word who appeared to Abraham as an angel, and that called to him not to hurt his son when he was about to sacrifice him [*On Dreams* 1.193-94].
4. It was the Word who appeared to Hagar [*On the Cherubim* 3; *On Dreams* 1.239-40].
5. It was the Word who appeared so many times to Jacob, though he is called the Angel that delivered him out of all his trouble [*Allegorical Interpretation* III 177]. It was the Word who appeared to Jacob in Bethel [*On the Migration of Abraham* 4-6; *On Dreams* 1.189-90], afterwards directed him how to manage Laban's flock [*On Dreams* 189-90] and advised him to return to the land of his kindred [*On Dreams* 189-90]. It was the Word who appeared to

Jacob in the form of an angel, and wrestled with him [*On Dreams* 128-29], and changed his name into that of Israel [*On the Changes of Names* 13.87; *On Dreams* 128-29].

6. It was the image of God, which in other places is the same with the Word, that appeared to Moses in the bush [*On the Life of Moses* 12.66]. It was God that called to him at the same time [*On Dreams* 1.194], even the Word [*On Dreams* 1.190-91] whom Moses desired to see [*Allegorical Interpretation* III.100-103].

7. It was the Word who led Israel through the wilderness (Ex 23) [*On Agriculture* 12.51]. He was the Angel in whom God placed his name [*On the Migration of Abraham* 31.174]. That Word who is called the Prince of angels, who was within the cloud [*The Heir of All Things* 42.205], and is called "Divine appearance of fire" [*On the Life of Moses* 46.254]. And he was this Angel that appeared to Moses and the elders of Israel on mount Sinai (Ex 24) [*On the Confusion of Tongues* 20.96; *On Dreams* I.11.62]. It was the Word whom those Jews rejected when they said, let us make a captain, and return into Egypt (Num 14) [*Allegorical Interpretation* III.61.175].

8. It was the Word who governs the world, that appeared to Balaam like an angel [*On Cherubim* 10.31-33; *On the Unchangeableness of God* 37.181].

9. It was the Word by whom Moses when he was to die was translated [*Sacrifices of Abel and Cain 3.8*].

II. Let us come next to the Chaldee paraphrases, and see how they render those texts that speak of the Divine appearances in Scripture; and let the reader take these remarks to heart,

1. That whatever he finds in those paraphrases, he may be assured that it was the general sense of the Jewish Church in ancient times.
2. That any judicious writer may justly suspect those who first published those Targums of having cut away their many parts in order to favor the new method of their last writers, which I have explained in the beginning of this chapter.

The first appearance of God to man was when he created our first parents (Gen 1:27). He blessed them and said to them, "*Be fruitful, and multiply, and replenish the earth*" (Gen 1:28). The one who gave them this blessing was the one who created them, as we read in the Jerusalem Targum on Gen 1:27, "*The Word of the Lord created man in his own image*." For his giving them the blessing, we have this in that Targum on Gen 35:9, "*O eternal God ... you have taught us the marriage-blessing of Adam and his wife; for thus the Scripture says expressly, 'And the Word of the Lord blessed them, and the*

Word of the Lord said to them, Be ye fruitful, and multiply, and replenish the earth.'"

God appeared again to our first parents after their sin where it is said, "*They heard the voice of the Lord God walking in the midst of the garden*" (Gen 3:8). Now as Philo said to us, it was the Word of the Lord who appeared to Adam; and both Onkelos and Jonathan agree that Adam and his wife "*heard the voice of the Word of the Lord God walking in the garden.*" Likewise in the Jerusalem Targum (vs. 9) it is said, "*The Word of the Lord called to Adam...,*" and again (vs. 10) where Adam makes this answer to God, "*I heard your voice in the garden;*" both Onkelos and Jonathan have it, "*I heard the voice of your Word in the garden.*"

In the history of the Deluge, we see that there was a revelation to Noah the preacher of righteousness to build the ark and to warn others while it was being built (1Pe 3:20). But who gave Noah that warning? Jonathan says, "*The Lord said this by his Word.*" And the Jerusalem Targum, "*It was the Word of the Lord that said this.*" And in the same way, Jonathan has it in Genesis 6:6 that, "*The Lord judged them by his Word;*" and said, "*I will destroy them by my Word.*" Likewise, for the saving of Noah all the paraphrasts attributed this to the Word: the Jerusalem Targum says, "*The Word of the Lord spared Noah*" (Gen 7:16). And in Gen 7:1 Jonathan has it, "*The Word of the Lord remembered Noah.*" Lastly, according to Onkelos and Jonathan,

"The Lord said by his Word, 'I will not again curse the ground any more for man's sake'" (Gen 8:21).

After the Flood God appeared often to Abraham. According to Jonathan on Genesis 15:6, a promise was made to Abraham that his seed should be as the stars of heaven for number, *"He believed in the Lord, and had faith in the (Memra) Word of the Lord,"* and it was counted to him for righteousness.[148] Therefore it was the Word of the Lord that came to him in a vision (15:1), and that made him that promise (5). It follows (7) that he said to Abraham, *"I am the Lord who brought you out of Ur of the Chaldees."* Who said this to Abraham? The Word of the Lord, according to Jonathan's Targum; for there is no other nominative case of the verb in his paraphrase. You see the same where Abraham divides the beasts in order to make a covenant with God. It was done at God's command, the one who afterward appeared between the pieces to Abraham and then solemnly entered into a covenant with him (Gen 15:9ff.). Here, says the Jerusalem paraphrase on Exodus 12:43, it was *"the Word of the Lord that appeared to Abraham between the pieces."* According to Onkelos and Jonathan, it was *"by his Word"* that God made this covenant with Abraham (Ex 6:8).

---

[148] This point is often missed by many. When Paul and James quote this verse about being justified by faith (Rom 4:9, 22; Gal 3:6; Jam 2:23), there is already a Christocentric, Word-oriented interpretation already present among the Jews. Who justified Abraham by faith? The Word. Who justifies us by faith? Christ Jesus. It's the same thing.

We must take notice that he who appeared then to Abraham says, "*I am El Shaddai*," which is translated, "*The Almighty God*," for according to Onkelos on Genesis 49:25, in the blessing of Jacob to his son Joseph, these names—*the Word of God* and *El Shaddai*, are parallel. Thus, it runs according to Onkelos, "*The Word of the God of your Father shall help you; and El Shaddai shall bless you*," where plainly *El Shaddai* is the same who is called, "*The Word of the God of your Father*."

As Philo taught us that the appearance of God to Abraham (Gen 18:1) was an appearance of the Word (*Allegorical Interpretation III*.217) where he calls one of the three angels that appeared to Abraham the *Logos*, the Word of God; and Josephus (1. 1. *Ant.* or *Antiquities of the Jews* 1.213) calls him God, so the Jerusalem paraphrase has it in the end of the next verse, "*The Word of the Lord appeared to Abraham in the valley of vision, as he sat warming himself in the sun, because of his circumcision.*" Elsewhere the same paraphrase quotes these words as being the words of Scripture saying, "*The Scripture has declared, 'And the Word of the Lord appeared to him in the valley of vision'*" (Gen 35:9). Jonathan also in his paraphrase on Deuteronomy 34:6 has these words, "*The Lord has taught us to visit the sick, in that he revealed himself by the vision of his Word to Abraham, when he was sick of the cutting of circumcision.*"

When God gave him a command for the sacrificing of his son (Gen 22:2) then, as Abraham was doing it, the Angel of the Lord called to him out of heaven, and told him, "*Now I know that you fear God, seeing you have not withheld your son, your only son, from ME.*" This last word plainly shows that this Angel was God himself, even the same that spoke to Abraham, and gave him that command (vs. 1, 2). And that command was given by the *Logos*, the Word, according to Philo, as it has been already shown. The Jerusalem paraphrase has the same in vs. 8 where, upon Isaac's inquiring for the lamb that was to be sacrificed, Abraham answered him, "*My son, the Word of the Lord will prepare me a sheep.*" And so, when Abraham found that the Word provided him a sheep and accepted that for a sacrifice instead of his son, "*Abraham worshipped, and prayed to the Word of the Lord, saying* (among many other things), '*You, O Lord, spoke to me, that I should offer up Isaac my son.*'"

In the other Targums (vv. 16-17), the Angel of the Lord calls to Abraham out of heaven the second time (the last word shows that this Angel was God himself; for it was God who called to him out of heaven the first time, as it has been already shown), and says to Abraham, "*By myself I have sworn, says the Lord. Because you have done this thing, and have not withheld your only son from me,*[149] *therefore in blessing I will bless you...*" There, both Onkelos and Jonathan say, "'*By my Word I have sworn,*' says the Lord." What should be

---

[149] *From Me* is in the Samaritan and LXX.

their meaning in this? When they say, "*Thus says the Lord*," it was properly used by the Word appearing here as an angel, and not according to his own natural being. But for the form of the oath, where, according to the Hebrew text (Gen 20), "*God swore by himself*," the paraphrasts render it that, "*God swore by his Word.*" and well they might, for they understood that the Word was God. And indeed, these Targums show in other places that where this form of swearing was used, it was the Word of the Lord who swore and held himself obliged to perform what was sworn (compare Ex 6:8 with Dt 26:5 and Num 14:30 with Dt 31:7).

We read of an Angel appearing to Hagar in the wilderness (Gen 16:7). He told her to return and submit to Sarah her mistress (9), telling her all about the child she now bore and what sort of man he would become. But as this Angel spoke in the style of God saying, "*I will greatly multiply your seed*" (10). So she confessed it was the Lord who spoke to her and she said to him, "*You, God, see me*" (13). It is clear that it was God himself who appeared, though he is called an Angel in the text. Therefore, not only does Philo call him the *Logos* in those places above mentioned, but the Targums likewise show that he was the Word of the Lord, according to the sense of the Jewish Church. Thus, Jonathan renders vs. 13, "*She confessed before the Lord Jehovah, whose Word had spoken to her;*" and the

Jerusalem Targum, "*She confessed and prayed to the Word of the Lord, who had appeared to her.*"

Again, an Angel called to Hagar out of heaven (Gen 21:16). But he also said to her that which no created angel could say; speaking of her son Ishmael, "*I will make him a great nation*" (18). Philo says that it was the *Logos*. And who performed this promise? It was God the Word, according to the Targums. For whereas the text says, "*God was with the lad;*" it is rendered both by Onkelos and Jonathan as, "*The Word of the Lord was his support or assistance*" (20).

We read also of two Divine appearances to Isaac, one in Gerar (Gen 26:2), and the other at Beersheba (24). In the former place, Isaac was ready to go down into Egypt, but God commanded him to continue in Canaan and gave him a promise in these words, "*I will be with you, and will bless you; for to you and your seed I will give all these countries, and I will perform the oath which I swore to Abraham your father*" (Gen 26:3). So then, he who appeared now to Isaac is the same who swore this to Abraham. So we learn much from this text. But according to the Targums, it was God the Word who swore all this to Abraham. Elsewhere they also tell us that it was the Word who swore to Isaac and to Abraham that he would give them the Promised Land (Ex 6:8; 32:13).

In the second appearance where God promised something to Isaac, he told him, "*I am the God of*

Abraham your father" (Gen 26:24). But the Jerusalem Targum says that, *"Abraham worshipped and prayed to the Word of the Lord"* (Gen 22:14). According to Jonathan's Targum, Isaac prayed for his son Jacob in these words, *"The Word of the Lord give you of the dew of heaven"* (Gen 27:28). In the same Targum on Genesis 31:5, where Scripture has Jacob saying, *"The God of my father has been with me,"* the Targum has, *"The Word of the God of my father,"*[150] or, *"The Word being the God of my father."*

Among the Divine appearances to Jacob, those two at Bethel were more remarkable than the rest: one at his going to Padan-Aram (Gen 28:13), the other at his return from there (Gen 35:9), where it is said expressly, *"then God appeared to him the second time."*

The history of the first of these is given us at large (Gen 28:13-16). Jacob himself gives this account of the last to his son Joseph (Gen 48:3-4). *"God Almighty appeared to me at Luz in the land of Canaan, and blessed me, and said to me, 'Behold, I will make you fruitful, and multiply you…"* That it was the Word who appeared to him, we have showed already from Philo in several places; and that this was the sense of the Jewish Church in his time, we have much reason to believe. As to this first appearance in the introduction (vs. 10), where the text speaks of Jacob's setting out from Beersheba to go to Haran, there both Jonathan and the Jerusalem

---

[150] *Of your father*; so the Samaritan and LXX.

Targum tell us of the sun set early that day because the Word[151] had a desire to speak with Jacob. Again, in the conclusion of this history (Gen 28:20-21), where Jacob vowed a vow saying, "*If God will be with me ... then shall the Lord be my God,*" here we read in Jonathan's Targum "*that Jacob vowed a vow to the Word, saying, 'If the Word of the Lord will be my help ... then the Lord will be my God.*"

Why should the paraphrast say that Jacob made this vow to the Word instead of God, as it is in the Hebrew text? Because they believed that it was the Word who appeared to him. Thus, who is the angel that spoke to Jacob (Gen 31:11)?[152] Where Scripture declares, "*I am the God of Bethel, where you vowed a vow to me*" (13), we see in the Targum on Genesis 28:20 that it was the Word to whom Jacob vowed a vow at Bethel. Therefore, according to this Targum, it must be the Word who is called an angel in this place.

The second time that God appeared to Jacob was in his return from Padan-Aram (Gen 35:9). It is expressly said in the Jerusalem Targum, "*The Word of the Lord appeared to Jacob the second time, when he was coming from Padan-Aram and blessed him,*" which is as clear a testimony as can be desired for our purpose.

---

[151] Jonathan has *Debbira* (Word) here. Scholars often note that *Memra* (Aramaic "Word") is used like John's *Logos*. But here, we have a synonym that is being used the same way.

[152] The sentence here, as well as the 1699 version, is unintelligible. It reads, "This being so, we cannot be to seek who that Angel was who spoke to Jacob..."

Whoever will consider with some attention those appearances of God to Jacob, and compare them with what we read in Genesis 18:15-16, and with what Hosea the Prophet says (Hos 12:3-4) concerning the Angel who was God, cannot but take notice of two things. The first is that the *Logos*, who is called an Angel, was indeed God. The second is, that the wrestling of that Angel with Jacob was a preparation for the belief of the mystery of the incarnation, by which the Apostles were made able to say, "*That which we have looked upon, and our hands have handled, of the Word of life—this is our message*" (1Jn 1:1, 5). But we must say more upon such an important subject.

CHAP. XIV.

That all the appearances of God, or of the Angel of the Lord, which are spoken of in Moses's time, have been referred to the Word of God by the ancient Jewish Church.

WE READ OF NO OTHER appearance of God, or of an Angel of the Lord, until Moses saw him on mount Horeb (Ex 3:2). There we read that *"the Angel of the Lord appeared to him in a flame of fire out of the midst of a bush."* This is the only place in this story where Moses calls him an Angel that appeared. Elsewhere he always calls him God, particularly in vs. 4, where he says that upon his turning aside to see why the bush did not burn, *"When the Lord saw this, God called to him out of the midst of the bush, and said to him, 'I am the God of your father, the God of Abraham, the God of Isaac, and the God of Jacob'"* (6). Upon seeing this sight, Moses says that he hid his face, for he was afraid to look upon God. After this, he goes on still calling him God, as we read in almost every verse. So, in vs. 16 he says, God commanded him to go to the elders of Israel, and say to them, *"The Lord God of your fathers, the God of Abraham, of Isaac, and of Jacob, appeared to me."* God would never have commanded him to tell them a lie, and therefore we may be sure that it was not a created angel, but God who appeared to him.

Why then should Moses once call him an Angel as we see he did in the second verse? A created angel he could not be, for the reasons now mentioned. He must therefore be God, and yet he must appear as an angel that came on a message from God. This is what Philo says in one word—he was the *Logos*, or Word, who is both God and the Messenger of God, as we have shown of him in several places.

As for the Targums, the matter is clear. For when Moses was sent to the children of Israel to tell them that their God had appeared to him and sent him to bring them forth out of Egypt, there Moses asked him his name. God said to Moses, "*Tell them, I AM THAT I AM*," or in fewer words, "*I AM has sent me to you.*" That which God calls himself here is the sense of the name Jehovah [Yahweh/LORD]; this signifies the Eternal Being. Now see how this is rendered in the Jerusalem Targum. There we read that "*the Word of the Lord said to Moses, 'He who said to the world, Let it be, and it was, and shall say to it again, Let it be, and it shall be.*" Here Moses asked God, and the Word answered his question. But it is certain that he who answered the question was the same Person who he had been speaking with all this time, even the same who appeared to him in the bush.

Moses being thus commissioned by the Word of God as his messenger to the children of Israel for the discharge of his ministry had both his instructions and credentials from the Word, according to the Targums.

For the first of these, God appeared to him more often than to anyone before him. R. Akiba (50-135 AD) said that Moses acted as mediator between the Gevura,[153] that is the Word of God, and the people of Israel, and observes that God spoke to him a hundred and seventy-five times. The times that God spoke to him from off the mercy-seat, upon the ark of testimony, and between the two cherubim were too many to count (Num 7:89). But those which R. Akiba reckons were appearances upon extraordinary occasions. In these two particular appearances, ordinary and extraordinary, it was the Word of God who spoke to Moses, according to the Targums.

Thus, they speak of God's talking to him from the mercy-seat and from there the Word was appointed to speak with him, according to Onkelos and Jonathan on Exodus 25:22 and 30:36. In Numbers 7:89, Jonathan says it was the Word who spoke to him. And likewise, in those occasional appearances both Jonathan and the Jerusalem Targums tell us once for all (Dt 34:10). *"The Word of the Lord knew Moses"* (*mmrl kl mmll qbvl*), to speak with him word for word.

---

[153] In Kaballah, the Gevura is one of ten Sefirot (emanations) through which the Ein Sof (Infinite) reveals itself and creates all things.

His credentials were all the signs and wonders which the Lord sent him to do (Dt 34:11); or, according to the Targums, which "*the Word of the Lord sent him to do, in Egypt, to Pharaoh, and his servants, and all his land; and in all that mighty land, and that great terror, which Moses showed in the sight of all Israel.*"

For the acts of his ministry, they were chiefly these three: 1. His bringing the people out of Egypt. 2. His giving them laws, and statutes, and judgments from God. 3. His leading them through the wilderness to the confines of Canaan. In each of these it was the Word who appeared to Moses, according to the Targums.

His bringing the people out of Egypt is wholly ascribed to the Word by Onkelos and Jonathan (Dt 20:1), and in Jonathan (Dt 24:18). The people were commanded to teach to their children that it was the Word of the Lord who did all those signs and wonders in Egypt, says Jonathan on Exodus 13:8. It was the Word who sent all those plagues on Pharaoh, and his servants, and all the land of Egypt, says Jonathan on Deuteronomy 29:1-2.[154] Especially, it was the Word who gave that stroke which finished the work, according to the Jerusalem Targum (Ex 12:29), namely, "*It was the Word of the Lord who appeared against the*

---

[154] Allix adds Dt 28:6, but I can find no close match to what this verse is supposed to say. However, this entire chapter is all about "the Word of the LORD" doing various things (see Dt 28:1, 7, 9, 11, 13, 15, 20, 21, 22, 25, 27, 28, 35, 45, 48, 49, 59, 61, 62, 63, 68).

Egyptians at midnight, and his right hand killed the firstborn of the Egyptians, and delivered his own firstborn the children of Israel."

After this, "*the Word of the Lord led the people through the desert to the Red sea,*" says the same Targum (Ex 13:18). "*The Word of the Lord, being their leader, in a pillar of fire by night, and of a cloud by day,*" says Onkelos (Dt 1:32-33). And when the people arrived at the Red sea, and they saw Pharaoh with his army behind them, they were in a rage against Moses and he cried to God (Ex 14:15). According to the Jerusalem Targum, "*The Word of the Lord said to Moses, 'How long will you stand and pray before me? — Tell the children of Israel to come forward, then reach out your rod and divide the Red sea.*" He did so, and according to the Jerusalem Targum on Dt 1:1, "*The Word divided the sea before them; so that the children of Israel went into the midst of the sea on dry ground*" (Ex 14:22), "*the Egyptians following them.*" And at morning, according to the Jerusalem Targum, "The Word of the Lord looked upon the army of the Egyptians, and threw upon them bitumen, and fire, and hail out of heaven" (24). And "*the Egyptians said, 'Let us fly from before the people of Israel, for this is the Word of the Lord that gets them victory'*" (25), but their flight was in vain, for "*by the Word of the Lord the waters were made heaps*" (Onkelos on Ex 15:8). And according to him also, when "*God spoke by his Word, the sea covered them*" (10). Thus, the whole work of the people of Israel's deliverance out of Egypt, every part of it, has been ascribed to the Word of the Lord by the Targums.

For the giving of the laws by which they were be formed into a Church and Kingdom; first, immediately after their coming out of the Red sea (Ex 15:25), according to the Jerusalem Targum, "*The Word of the Lord gave them precepts and orders of judgments,*" particularly, as Jonathan has it, "*The Word of the Lord gave them there the law of the sabbath, and that of honoring father and mother, and judgments concerning bruises and wounds, and for the punishment of transgressors.*" Afterwards, when they had come into the wilderness of Sinai, the text says, "*Moses went up to God, and the Lord called to him out of the mount, saying, 'Thus shall you say to the house of Israel...*" (Ex 19:3). There Onkelos says, according to one of Clark's[155] various readings, "*Moses went up to meet the Word of the Lord*" (Ex 19:8). Moses returns with the People's answer to the Lord, then, according to the Jerusalem Targum, "*The Word of the Lord said to Moses, 'Go to the people, and sanctify them today and tomorrow, and let them wash their clothes, and be ready for the third day, for the third day the Lord will come down in the sight of all the people upon mount Sinai*" (9). Accordingly, the people, having prepared themselves on the third day, according to Onkelos, "*Moses brought the people out of the camp to meet the Word of God*" (17), yet the people

---

[155] Samuel Clark (1626-1701). English Nonconformist, rector at Grendon Underwood, Buckinghamshire, and annotator of the Bible. He was a friend of John Owen, Richard Baxter, and George Whitefield.

only saw thunder and lightning and the mountain smoking and felt the earth quake under them. They also heard the noise of the trumpet, which so frightened them that they removed and stood at a distance and said to Moses, "*You speak to us, and we will hear; but do not let the Word from before the Lord speak with us, lest we die*" (Ex 20:19), according to Onkelos, in one of Clark's various readings. Moses therefore, according to Jonathan on Deuteronomy 5:5 "*stood between them and the Word of the Lord, to show them the Pithgama* [Pithgama is another Aramaic word for "word"], *the matter and words that were spoken to him from the Lord.*" What they were, we read in Exodus 20:1ff. where, according to the Jerusalem Targum, the Word of the Lord spoke the tenor of all these words, saying, "*I am the Lord your God, who brought you out of the land of Egypt, out of the house of bondage.*" After this follow the Ten Commandments, commonly called the Decalogue. That it was God the Word who spoke this to the people, the ancient Church could not doubt, as we see in the Book of Deuteronomy where Jonathan tells us that Moses reminded his people of what they had heard and saw at the giving of the Law (Dt 4:33). "*Is it possible that a people should have heard the voice of the Word of the Lord, the living God, speak out of the middle of the fire, as you have heard, and yet live?*" Again, vs. 36, "*Out of heaven he has made you hear the voice of his Word, — and you have heard his words out of the midst of the fire.*"

Again, he puts them in mind of the fright they were in (Dt 5:23). "*After you had heard the voice of the Word out of the midst of the darkness on the mount burning with fire, all your chiefs came to me, and said, 'Behold, the Word of the Lord our God has shown us the Divine Majesty of his glory, and the excellence of his magnificence, and we have heard the voice of his Word out of the midst of the fire, why should we die, as we must, if we hear any more of the voice of the Word of the Lord our God; for who is there living in flesh, that hears the voice of the Word of the living God speaking out of the middle of the fire, as we do, and yet live?*" Again, in Deuteronomy 18:16 he reminds them of the same thing in some of the same words. Many more such quotations might be added, but these are sufficient to prove that it was the undoubted tradition of the ancient Jewish Church that their Law was given by the Word of God and that it was he who appeared to Moses for this purpose.

As the Word gave the Law, it was also he who made promises in those many appearances to Moses throughout his whole leading of the people of Israel through the wilderness.

I will begin with that Divine appearance, which was continually in sight of all the people of Israel for forty years together throughout their whole travel in the wilderness; namely, the pillar which they saw in the air day and night. In the place this pillar is first spoken of, namely, at the coming of the people of

Israel up out of Egypt, there it is expressly said that *"the Lord went before them in the pillar of cloud by day, and fire by night"* (Ex 13:21). Afterward, he is called the Angel of God (Ex 14:19), where we read that the people, having come to the Red Sea and being in imminent danger of being overtaken by the Egyptians by whom they were closely pursued, the Angel who had gone before the camp of Israel all day, turned at night and went behind them. That this Angel was God is certain, not only because he is called God[156] (Ex 13:21; 14:24; Num 12:5), but also because he was worshipped (Ex 33:10), which was a sure proof of his Divinity. Since he was God himself, and yet the Messenger [Angel] of God, it must be that this was the *Logos* or Word; and that this was the tradition of the ancient Church, we are taught not only by Philo in the place mentioned above,[157] but also by the Jerusalem Targum on Ex 14:24, and Jonathan on Ex 33:9, and by Onkelos on Dt 1:32-33, as has been mentioned.

When the children of Israel, after the first three days' march, found no other waters but those that were too bitter for them to drink, at which time they murmured, Moses cried to the Lord, who immediately showed him a tree, which they threw into the waters to make them sweet (Ex 15:25). Here was a

---

[156] Technically, he is called Yahweh.
[157] *On Husbandry* 51; *The Heir of All Things* 42.201-205.

Divine appearance and it was of the Word of the Lord, according to the Jerusalem Targum.

A month after their coming out of Egypt, they murmured for lack of bread against Moses and Aaron; at which time God showed himself so much concerned that *he made his glory appear to them in the cloud* (Ex 16:7, 10). That according to the sense of the ancient Church, this was the *Shekinah* of the Word, has been just now shown, both from Philo and from all the Targums; and we find the same here in this place where Moses tells them, "*Your murmurings are not against us, but against the Word of the Lord*" (vs. 8), according to Onkelos and Jonathan.

When the Amalekites came against this poor people that had never seen war (Ex 17:8ff.), and smote those at the rear, God not only gave his people a victory over them, but also said to Moses, "*Write this for a memorial in a book ... that I will utterly blot out the memory of Amalek from under heaven*" (Ex 17:14). What did Moses then do? In the place where they had fought, he set up an altar with *Jehovah-Nissi*, "*The Lord is My Banner*" (15), meaning that it was the will of God they should be in perpetual war against Amalek. He recorded this reason for it in his book according to Jonathan, "*For the Word of the Lord has sworn by his glory, that he will have war against Amalek for all generations*" (16).

The next Divine appearance we read of was at the giving of the Law on mount Sinai; where we have already said enough, and we must avoid being too long. For this reason, we omit much more that might be said of the following appearances in the wilderness, which are all ascribed to the Word in one or another of the Targums. But I ought not to fail to take notice of some special things.

For their places of worship, God promised according to the Jerusalem Targum, "*In every place that you remember my Name in prayer, I will be revealed to you in my Word and I will bless you,*" and the temple is called "*the place which the Word of the Lord your God will choose to place his Shekinah there,*" according to Jonathan's and the Jerusalem Targums on Deuteronomy 12:5 and Exodus 20:24. Especially at the altar for sacrifice, which was before the door of the tabernacle, God promised Moses, both for himself and the people, according to Onkelos and Jonathan on Exodus 29:42, "*I will appoint my Word to speak with you there, and I will appoint my Word there for the children of Israel.*" Above all, at the mercy seat where the ark stood, God promised to Moses, according to those Targums on Exodus 25:22 and 30:6,[158] "*I will appoint my Word to speak with you there.*" In sum of all the precepts in Leviticus, it is said at the end of that book, according to those

---

[158] Original reads 30:36. This is a typo. Numbers 27:4 is inexplicable, so I have removed it.

Targums, "*These are the statutes and judgments and laws which the Lord made between his Word and the children of Israel*" (Lev 26:46).

When they entered into covenant with God, obliging themselves to live according to his laws, they made the Word to be their King and themselves his subjects. So Moses tells them, according to the Jerusalem Targum, "*This day you have made the Word of the Lord King over you so that he may be your glory*" (Dt 26:17). And, "*The Word of the Lord rules over you as king this day, as over his beloved and peculiar people*" (18). As a consequence of being their King, he ordered them by his chief minister Moses to make him a royal pavilion or tabernacle, and to set it up in the midst of their camp. Both that and all of its furniture he ordered Moses to make according to the pattern showed him in the mount (Ex 25:40). Especially for the presence of the great King, there was to be an apartment in the inner part of the tabernacle separated from the rest with a veil embroidered with cherubim (Ex 27:31). This part was called the Most Holy Place, or the Holy of Holies (Ex 27:33).

Here the ark was to be placed, overlaid with pure gold and having a crown of gold round about it. In the ark was contained the tablets of the Law. Upon it was placed the mercy-seat, overshadowed with the wings of two cherubim that stood on the two ends of the mercy-seat (Ex 37:9), each one looking at the other and both of them toward the mercy-seat.

This provision was being made for the place of his *Shekinah*, the Word, who showed himself before in a cloudy pillar by day, and in a fiery pillar by night that stood over the camp. Now from here, he came to take possession of his royal seat in the tabernacle over the ark; from where, out of the void space between these cherubim it was that the Word used to speak to Moses and to give him orders from time to time for the government of his people, according to the paraphrasts on Ex 25:22 and 30:6,[159] and especially Num 7:89, as mentioned above.

From here on out, throughout their whole journey through the wilderness, the pillar was constantly over the tabernacle, and the people attended him. But whenever he gave the commandment, the pillar moved and showed which way the camp was to go. Upon notice of that, Moses first gave the word in a set form of prayer, which we have in the first six verses of the 68th Psalm. The first verse of it is in Numbers 10:35 in these words, according to the Jerusalem Targum, "*Arise now, O Word of the Lord, in the might of your strength.*"[160] According to Jonathan's paraphrase, "*Appear now, O Word of the Lord, in the strength of your wrath.*" In both the Targums it follows, as in the

---
[159] See note above.
[160] Psalm 68. "*To the choirmaster. A Psalm of David. A Song. God shall arise, his enemies shall be scattered.*"

Hebrew text, "*And the enemies of your people he shall scatter, and they that hate you shall flee before you.*" When they had performed their journey according to the will of their King, which they knew by seeing the pillar stand still, then Moses used the form for the resting of the ark. According to the forementioned Targums, "*Return now, O Word of the Lord, to your people Israel; make the glory of your Shekinah dwell among them and have mercy on the thousands of Israel*" (Num 10:36). After this was said, the priests (who carried the several pins of the tabernacle) laid down their burdens and set up all things as before; then the pillar returned to its place over the midst of the tabernacle.

In this state of Theocracy, their keeping of God's laws is called by their Targums "*the believing and obeying of the Word.*" Their breaches of his laws are called "*their despising and rebelling against the Word.*" Of the use of both these manners of speaking there might be given more instances than can be easily numbered.

The Targums likewise ascribe to the Word both the rewarding of their obedience and the punishing of their transgressions. On their obedience, according to the Targums, it was the usual promise that the Word should be their help or support (Num 23:8, 21); that he should bless them and multiply them (Dt 24:19); that he should rejoice over them to do them good (Dt 28:63, 30:9). They were told that he would be "*a consuming fire to their enemies*" (Dt 4:24); particularly, that he was so to the Anakims (Dt 9:3); that *"it was he that delivered Og into their hands"* (Dt 3:2); that *"it was he that would cast out all the nations before them"* (Dt 9:23).

On the other hand, according to the sense of the ancient Church, it was the Word who punished them for their disobedience, and also it was he who forgave them upon their repentance. Of both these kinds there are many remarkable instances, as particularly, of the punishing of their disobedience. According to Jonathan on Exodus 32:35, it was the Word who destroyed the people for worshipping the calf that Aaron made. For their lusting at Kibroth-hattaava, Moses told them who it was whom they provoked by it (Num 11:20). (According to Onkelos and Jonathan,) *"You have despised the Word of the Lord, whose Shekinah dwells among you."*

Because of their refusal to go forward into the Promised Land, because of the evil report of the spies, Moses tells them, according to those Targums, *"It was rebelling against the Word of the Lord"* (Dt 1:26). Afterward, when they went up contrary to God's decree, Moses asks them, *"Why do you transgress the decree of the Word of the Lord?"* (Num 14:41). In their murmuring at Zalmona, according to Onkelos in one Polyglot of Clark's various readings, *"They spoke against the Word of the Lord, and against Moses."*[161] Thus, Num 21:6 according to the Jerusalem Targum, *"The Word of the*

---

[161] Polyglot vol. 4.

Lord sent fiery serpents among the people." Upon their whoring with Baal-Peor, according to the Jerusalem Targum, "*The Word of the Lord said to Moses, 'Take all the heads of the people, and hang them up before the Lord'*" (Num 25:4).[162] In short, according to the Targums on Deuteronomy 28:20ff., it was "*the Word of the Lord*" who would send all his judgments and curses that are there denounced against impenitent sinners.

But on the other hand, according to those Targums, it belonged to "*the Word*" to grant pardon to those who were qualified for it. So when Moses begged pardon for his people that had sinned beyond mercy, if it had not been infinite, according to the Jerusalem Targum, "*The Word of the Lord answered him, and said, 'Behold, I have forgiven, and pardoned according to your word'*" (Num 14:20). In case that, upon the inflicting of God's judgments mentioned above, God's people should be brought to repentance, it was promised, according to Jonathan's Targum, that "*then the Word should accept their repentance according to his good pleasure, and should have mercy on them, and gather them out of all nations…*" (Dt 30:3). So likewise 32:36, according to the same Targum, it is promised that "*the Word of the Lord judges mercifully the case of his people, and there will be pity before him for the evil that he will decree upon his servants.*" It would be very easy to add many more such instances out of the Targums; but these are

---

[162] Or "*You shall crucify them on wood before the Word of the Lord.*"

abundantly enough to show the sense of the ancient Church, what they thought of him who so often appeared to their fathers in the wilderness, and spoke to them by his servant Moses.

When Moses understood that God would not let him live to bring his people into the Promised Land; he implored God to send him a successor, in these words, according to Jonathan's Targum, "*Let the Word of the Lord, who has dominion over the souls of men … appoint a faithful man over the congregation of his people*" (Num 27:16). Moses gave him this charge to Joshua, God having appointed Joshua in his stead, in the hearing of the people, according to Onkelos and Jonathan, "*Your eyes have seen what the Lord did to Og and Sihon, so he will do to all the kingdoms that you pass through; therefore do not fear them, for the Word of the Lord your God shall fight for you*" (Dt 3:21-22).

He repeated the same thing later to all the people; telling them first, according to Jonathan, "*The Word of the Lord said to me, 'You shall not pass over this Jordan, but the Lord your God and his Shekinah will go before you'*" (Dt 31:2-3). He adds, "*And Joshua will go over before you, as the Lord has spoken*" (4). And regarding all your enemies, "*the Word of the Lord shall deliver them up before you*" (5). Therefore, it says in Onkelos, "*Do not fear them, for the Word of the Lord your God goes before you; he will not fail nor forsake you*" (6).

After this, Moses calls to Joshua and says to him in front of them all, according to Jonathan, "*Be strong and of a good courage, you must go with this people into the land which the Word of the Lord has sworn to their fathers that he would give them ... and the Shekinah of the Word of the Lord shall go before you, and his Word shall be your help; he will not leave you nor forsake you. Do not fear, neither be dismayed*" (7-8). He repeats it again from God to Joshua, according to Onkelos and Jonathan, "*You shall bring the children of Israel into the land which I have sworn to them; and my Word will be your help*" (23).

It was on that same day that he gave this charge to Joshua that Moses also gave them his prophetic song (22-23). God then told Moses that same day, "*Go up to ... mount Nebo, and die*" (32:48-49). Moses obeyed and lingered no longer than to give the tribes of Israel his blessing before his death (33:1). When this was finished, he went up to mount Nebo (34:1). There, according to Jonathan, it was "*the Word of the Lord*" who gave satisfaction to his bodily eyes to see all the land of Canaan before they were closed. So, vs. 5, "*Moses the servant of the Lord died there ... according to the Word of the Lord.*" He was translated by the *Logos*, according to Philo.[163] It was certainly the current tradition of the Church in his age that his soul was taken out of his body "*by a kiss of the Word of the Lord,*" as Jonathan

---

[163] *The Sacrifices of Abel and Cain* 3.8.

renders it; or, according to the Jerusalem Targum "*at the mouth of the decree of the Word of the Lord.*"

After his death, Joshua took up the reigns of leadership, and according to the Jerusalem Targum, "*The children of Israel obeyed Joshua, and they did as the Word of the Lord had commanded Moses*" (9).

Besides all these Divine appearances to Moses and the children of Israel, there are also a few that were made to Balaam on their account and are therefore recorded in the same sacred history. Where these are first mentioned, both Onkelos and Jonathan have, "*The Word came from before the Lord to Balaam, 'Who are these men who are with you?'*" (Num 22:9). So again, the second time, according to the same Targums, "*The Word came from before the Lord to Balaam by night, and said to him, 'If these men have come to call you…'*" (20). It is plain that the ancient Jewish Church took these appearances to have been made by the Word.

But what opinion did they have of the Angel's appearing to Balaam (vs. 22)? Others may ask what they thought of the dialogue between Balaam and the donkey that he rode upon, which occurred because the beast was frightened at the Angel's appearing to him. All this, as Maimonides says, happened only in vision of prophecy.[164] But it was a thing that really happened, we are assured by St. Peter who tells us, "*God opened the mouth of the dumb beast to rebuke the*

---

[164] Maim. *More Nebochim* 11. P. 42.

madness of the Prophet" (2Pe 2:16). As it cannot be doubted that Balaam used to have communication with devils that spoke to him in various ways, so there is reason to believe they spoke to him sometimes by the mouth of dumb beasts. If so, then to hear the donkey speak could not be strange to him. And why God should order it so? There is a reason given in Jonathan and the Jerusalem Targum. The reader may see other reasons elsewhere, but they are not proper for this place.[165]

We need to consider whether this angel that appeared to Balaam was a created angel or not. It appears by the words to have been the Lord himself who appeared as an angel to Balaam; for thus he says to him, "*Go with the men, but speak only the word that I tell you*" (Num 22:35). Now it does not appear after this that anyone else spoke to him from God, but God himself. Therefore, Philo says plainly that this appearance was of the *Logos*, as has been already shown. And that this was the sense of the Church in his age, we may see in the two following appearances to Balaam, as well as in the two that were before this. The Targums say it was "*the Word who met Balaam, and spoke to him*" (Thus, both Onkelos and Jonathan on Num 23:4, 16).

---

[165] *Muis Varis*, p. 95.

CHAP. XV.

That all the appearances of God, or of the Angel of the Lord, which are spoken of in the books of the Old Testament after Moses's time, have been referred to the Word of God by the Jews before Christ's incarnation.

Thus far it has been our business to show that it was the Word who made all those appearances, either of God or of an Angel of God that was worshipped, in any part of the five books of Moses. We have been much larger in this than was necessary for our present occasion. But whatever may seem to have been over-kill in the previous chapter, it is hoped the reader will not wish we had said less, when he comes to reflect upon the use of it, to prove that the Word was a Person and that he was God.

Now, we will try to make amends for the wordiness used previously through the shortness of what we have to say in the rest of this chapter. We will look at those Divine appearances that are recorded in the other books of Scripture after the Pentateuch, and we will find those appearances fewer and fewer, until they basically come to cease in the Jewish Church. For once the *Logos* was settled as the King of Israel between the cherubim, he was not to be looked for in other places. Of those books of Scripture in which the following appearances are mentioned, we do not have as many paraphrases as we had for the five books of Moses.[166] One paraphrase is all that we have of most of the books we now speak of. Yet, we have reason to thank God, that that evidence of the Divine appearances of the Word of God have been so abundantly sufficient, that we have no need for anymore. In what will see in the following appearances of God, or the Angel who was worshipped, it will be enough to show that the ancient Jewish Church had the same notion that they had of those already mentioned out of the five books of Moses.

We read of but one Divine appearance to Joshua, and that is when a man with a drawn sword in his hand came to him, calling himself the captain of the Lord's host (Josh 5:13-14). Some would say that this was a created angel, but certainly Joshua did not take him for one. Otherwise he would not have fallen down on his face and worshipped him as he did (14). Nor would a created angel have received it from him without reproving him, as the angel did to St. John in a similar situation (Rev 19:10; 22:9). But this Divine Person was so far from admonishing him for having done too

---

[166] Genesis-Deuteronomy have three Targums: Onkelos, Jerusalem/Neofiti, and Pseudo-Jonathan. Most of the other books only have one.

much that he commanded him to keep going and do even more, requiring of him the highest acknowledgment of a Divine Presence that was in use among the eastern nations. We see this in these words, *"Take off your sandals from your feet, for the place where you are standing is holy"* (Josh 5:15).

Now, considering that these are the exact same words that God said to Moses in Exodus 3:2-3, we see a plain reason why God should command this to Joshua. It was for the strengthening of his faith, to let him know that as he was now in Moses's role, so God would be the same to him that he had been to Moses. This is particularly so with respect to that trial which required a more than ordinary measure of faith, that is the difficult task of taking the stronghold of Jericho with such an army as he had without any provision for a siege. Thus, the Lord said to him, *"See, I have given Jericho into your hand"* (Josh 6:2). No one but God could say and do this; and the text plainly says, *"It was the Lord."* That the Lord who thus appeared as a warrior and called himself *"the captain of the Lord's host,"* was none other than the Word, as was plainly the sense of the ancient Jewish Church. This appears in what remains of it in their paraphrase on Joshua 10:14, *"For the Lord the God of Israel by his Word waged battle for Israel."* It is also found in later, *"For the Lord your God—his Word—was fighting for you"* (23:3, 10), and also vs. 13 which says, "*It was the Word who cast out the nations before them.*"

Indeed, this very judgment of the old synagogue is to be seen not only in their Targums until this day, but in their most ancient books (*Rabboth*, fol. 108. col. 3.; *Zohar*, par. 3. fol. 139. col. 3.; Tanch. *ad Exod.* iii.; Ramb. *ad Exod.* iii., Bach. fol. 69. 2). The learned Masius in Joshua 5:13-14 has translated the words of Ramban,[167] and he has preferred his interpretation, which is the most ancient amongst the Jews, to the sense of the commentators of the Church of Rome.[168]

As for divine appearances in the Book of Judges, we read of one to Gideon that seems to have been of an angel of God, for so he is called (Jdg 6:11-12, 20-22). In this last place it is also said that "*Gideon perceived he was an Angel of the Lord.*" That is, he saw that this was a heavenly person that came to him with a message from God. And yet that he was no created angel it seems, because he is so often simply called the Lord (14, 16, 23, 24, 25, 27). Gideon in that whole story never addressed himself to anyone other than God. The message delivered from God by this Angel to Gideon is thus rendered in the Targum, "*Surely my Word shall be you help, and you shall smite the Midianites as one man*" (16). The Word who helped Gideon against the Midianites was none other than he who

---
[167] Moses ben Nahman.
[168] Given that Masius was a Roman priest, this is remarkable.

appeared to Joshua with a sword in his hand (Josh 5:13). This was now the sword of the Lord and of Gideon (Jdg 7:18, 20).

What the ancient Jewish Church meant by the Word of the Lord in this place one may guess by their Targum on Judges 6:12-13, where the angel says to Gideon, "*The Word of the Lord is at your aid, O mighty warrior.*" And Gideon said to him: "*Please, master, if the Shekinah of the Lord has come to our aid, why has all this happened to us?*" It is plain by this paraphrase that they reckoned the Word of the Lord to be identical with the *Shekinah* of the Lord, even he by whom God had so gloriously appeared for their deliverance. And indeed they could hardly be mistaken in the person of that Angel who says that his name is *Pele*, the Wonderful, which is used among the names of the Messiah (Isaiah 9:6), which name the Jews make a shift to appropriate to God, exclusively to the Messiah.

The angel who appeared to Manoah (Judges 13) could seem to have been none other than a created angel. But the name which he takes of *Pele*, The Wonderful, shows that he was the Word of the Lord, or the Angel of the Lord (Isa 63:8).

In the first Book of Samuel we read of no other such appearance, except that which God made to Samuel (1Sa 3:21). This was only by "*a voice from the temple of the Lord, where the ark was at that time*" (3-4). The word *hekal* signifies a temple or a palace, thus the tabernacle was called where the ark was in those days at Shiloh. It was there that "*God revealed himself to Samuel by the Word of the Lord*" (21). But that the Word of the Lord was their King, and the tabernacle was his palace, where his throne was upon the ark between the cherubim, and that from this place the Word gave his oracle in the opinion of the ancient Jewish Church, all this has been so fully proved in the previous chapters, such that to prove it here again would be superfluous. Therefore, I take it for granted that, in their opinion, it was the Word of the Lord from whom this voice came to Samuel.

In the second Book of Samuel we read how, upon David's sin in numbering the people, God sent the Prophet Gad to give him his choice of three punishments: either three years of famine, or three months of destruction by enemies, or three days of pestilence throughout all the coast of Israel. This last one was a judgment from heaven that would fall equally upon a prince or a peasant. And so David made this his choice, rather than of either of the other two. He said, "*Do not let me fall into the hands of man, but rather into the hands of the Lord. For great are his mercies*" (1Ch 21:13). Thus, God sent a pestilence upon all the coasts of Israel and seventy thousand men fell (2Sa 24:15).

To prove to David's bodily eyes this extraordinary instance, as well as God's justice in punishing sinners, and his mercy to them if they repented and prayed, God made him see an angel standing between the earth and the heaven, having a drawn sword in his hand stretched out over Jerusalem to destroy it (2Sa 24:16-17; 1Ch 21:16). When David saw this sight, he fell on his face and prayed. Then God said to the destroying angel, "*It is enough, stay now your hand. Then the angel came down and stood by the floor of Oman the Jebusite*" (2Sa 24:16). (This was on the very place God designed that Solomon should build his temple and he declared it to David at this occasion). There, according to the angel's order by the Prophet Gad, David now built an altar, and sacrificed upon it. Then, "*The Lord commanded the angel, and he put his sword into his sheath*" (17). This was none other than a created angel, whom God employed into his service and appointed to appear in that manner for all those purposes mentioned.[169]

What the ancient Church thought of all this passage of history, we may easily guess by what has already been shown of their ascribing all rewards and punishments to the Word who had the management and government over God's people. And though it seems that care has been taken to conceal this notion

---

[169] What Allix says in this sentence is difficult to understand. Is he saying that he believes the angel in this text was created? If so, it why bring this story up? Is he saying that the OT church believed this angel was created? This seems to put the cart before the horse, for he will immediately say that later Jews appear to have tried to conceal the early understanding but have failed to fully eradicate all vestiges of the Word in this story. This means he is proving from this passage that this Angel was in fact the Word, which is consistent with his entire argument.

of theirs as much as was possible in the Targums of the books now before us; yet there is a passage that seems to have escaped the correctors, by which we may perceive that the sense of the Church here was agreeable to what we find of it in all other places. For in 2 Samuel 24:14, where we find in the text that David said, "*Let us fall now into the hand of the Lord, for his mercies are great,*" the Targum renders these words, "*Let me be delivered into the hand of the Word of the Lord, for great are his mercies.*" It was therefore the Word of the Lord into whose hands David fell. It was his Angel by whom the judgment was executed; and it was also his mercy by which the judgment was suspended and revoked. The Targum on this text sufficiently shows that all this was the sense of the Jewish Church.

In short, the ancient Church considered the Word as being their Sovereign Lord, and King of the people of Israel. All those kings whose acts are described in the two Books of Kings, they looked upon them as his lieutenants or deputies, who held their title from and under him by virtue of his covenant with David their father. Solomon declares this in these words, "*Blessed be the Lord God of Israel, who by his Word made a covenant with David my father*" (1Kg 8:15). Whatever God did for his people under their government, in protecting and delivering them from their enemies, they owned that it was "*for his Word's sake, and for his servant David's sake*" (2Kg 19:34; 20:6).

When they had broken his covenant, God removed them from before his Word, and gave them up to be a scorn to all nations, as he threatened he would do (1Kg 9:7, according to their Targum).

In these books we read of only two more divine appearances in Solomon's time, and both these to Solomon himself (1Kg 9:2).

The first was at Gibeon (1Kg 3:5), where the Lord appeared to Solomon "*in a dream by night,*" and said to him, "*Ask what I shall give you.*" He asked nothing but wisdom, which so pleased the Lord that he gave him not only that but also riches and honor above all the kings then in the world. The Targum, as it has come to our hands, does not say it was the Word of the Lord that appeared to him, and that gave him all this. But that it was so according to the sense of their Church may be gathered from the text, which tells us that as soon as Solomon was awake, he went immediately to Jerusalem (which was about seven miles distant) and there "*he stood before the ark of the covenant of the Lord*" (which was there in the tabernacle set up by David his father), "*and he offered up both burnt offerings and peace offerings, and made a feast to all his servants*" (15). The haste in which all this was done brings us to the reason he did this. For of all peace offerings for thanksgiving to God, the same day that they were offered, the flesh had to be eaten (Lev 7:15). The breast and the right shoulder by the priests, all the rest by the offeror and those that he had to eat with him. It is plain, therefore, that this was a sacrifice of thanksgiving to God. But why did Solomon not stay in Gibeon and pay his duty at the place where he had received the vision, especially since the tabernacle which Moses made by God's command, and the brazen altar which Bezaleel made (2Ch 1:2-4), and more were all there at Gibeon? It is because Solomon had come on purpose to Gibeon to sacrifice upon that altar at that time in the first place. The very day before this appearance of God, he had offered a thousand burnt offerings upon it (6), and on that very night God appeared to him (7). Now given that Solomon had found such good success when he sacrificed at Gibeon that God came and appeared to him and gave him so great a blessing, we would think he would certainly have stayed there to have paid his thanksgiving in that place. But instead, he understood that the one who appeared to him was the Word, and his special presence was with the ark at Jerusalem, as we have abundantly proved. Therefore, he quickly hurried to that place to pay his burnt offerings and peace offerings of thanksgiving to the Word of the Lord. This we cannot doubt was the sense of the ancient Jewish Church, though it doth not appear now in their Targums.

If it was the Word who made that first appearance to Solomon, then it must be he who made the second also. For both of these appearances were by the same person. So, it is said expressly in the text, "*The Lord appeared to Solomon the second time, as he had appeared to him at Gibeon*" (1Kg 9:2). But of this second appearance, that it was the Word of the Lord, there is a clearer proof than of first; as the reader will certainly judge, if he considers the circumstances of this second appearance and the words which God spoke to Solomon on this occasion.

First, the time of this divine appearance to Solomon was when he had finished the building of the house of the Lord (1). He had brought the ark into the most holy place, even under the wings of the cherubim (1Kg 8:6). The glory of the Lord had taken possession of this house (10-11), and Solomon had made his prayer and supplication before it (12-61). Subsequently, God appears and tells him, "*I have heard the prayer and supplication that you have made before me. I have hallowed this house which you have built*" (9:3). That is, I have taken it for my own, "*to put my name there forever*" (1Ch 7:12). "*I have chosen this place to myself for a house of sacrifice.*" This was a plain declaration from God, that it was of this house that he had spoken by Moses in these words, "*There shall be a place which the Lord your God shall choose to place his name there, here shall you bring all that I command you, your burnt offerings and your sacrifices*" etc. (Dt 12:5, 11). Now see how those words of Moses are rendered in Jonathan's Targum on Deuteronomy, "*There will be a place which the Word of the Lord will choose to place his Shekinah, there shall you bring your offerings*" etc. Here we cannot but see that he that appeared to Solomon and said to him, "*I have chosen this place*" etc. Speaking all along in the first person is the same one of whom Moses said all the same things but spoke of him in the third person. As it appears in Jonathan's Targum (both vs. 5. and 11) of that chapter, this was none other than the Word, according to the doctrine of the ancient Jewish Church; though in their Targum on 1 Kings 9 (which also is called Jonathan's, but how truly the reader may see by this instance) there is not the least mention of the Word upon this occasion.

The Word of the Lord now resting at his place in Solomon's temple (2Ch 6:41), and having put an end to his own theocracy by setting up kings of Solomon's lineage that came in by hereditary succession and governed after the manner of the kings of other nations; after this, in the Scripture history of those times, while the first temple was standing, we read of no more divine appearances as we formerly had.

There is only one exception, namely, that when Elijah heard that "*still small voice*" (1Kg 19), of which something ought to be said more particularly. It may be observed that this was in that part of Israel which had no communion with the temple. It was in Ahab's time, when the children of Israel had not only cast off the seed of David but seemed to have quite forsaken the covenant which God had made with their fathers by his servant Moses. To bring them back to their duty, God had now sent Elijah, who was a kind of second Moses. God showed this by putting him into so many of Moses's circumstances. For example, after a fast of forty days, which no one except Moses had ever kept before him, he comes to Horeb, the mount of God (1Kg 19:8).

We first read of this mountain in Exodus 3:1, when God first appeared to Moses at this same place. There (Ex 3:6), Moses hid his face because he was afraid to look upon God. Elijah did the same thing in this same place (1Kg 19:13). He wrapped his face in his cloak and then God spoke to him, just as he had done first to Moses. He who spoke now was the same who spoke then. This is made clear by comparing the circumstances. He who spoke then was God the Word, as we have proved before in the former chapter. This was the sense of the ancient Jewish Church. And to us Christians, it cannot but look very agreeable that just as when Moses and Elijah were upon the earth, the Word appeared to them and spoke with them on mount Horeb; so also when he was made flesh and dwelt among us, Moses and Elijah came to him on mount Tabor[170] and spoke with him at his transfiguration.

---

[170] There is good reason to believe this was actually on Mt. Hermon. The text does not say, but it is clear that they were just at Caesarea Philippi, which is at the base of Mt. Hermon.

Of those appearances of angels to Elijah (1Kg 19:5, 7; 2Kg 1) and the angel who slaughtered so many of Sennacherib's army (2Kg 19:35), we have no more to say in this place; because they seem to have been created angels, and neither of them is called the Word of the Lord in their Targum.

But we can say something about that vision of God which was seen by the prophet Micaiah (1Kg 22:19ff.). Although he does not say that God appeared to him, nor that he saw anything more of God than a mere resemblance of a king sitting in state, which was at that moment visibly represented before him, we must take notice of one thing. It is of some importance that when he says, "*I saw the Lord sitting on his throne, and all the host of heaven standing by him on his right hand and on his left*" etc., the most learned Jews conceive that he saw the *Shekinah* with the angels of his attendance, and that this vision of Micaiah is the same which was showed to Isaiah (Isa 6:1ff.), and to some of the other prophets.

In the prophetical books of Isaiah and Ezekiel, there are two appearances of God, or of the *Shekinah* in his temple, which we are obliged to give some account. Of these, as I will show, we have no reason to doubt but that it was the Word who appeared to those prophets according to the sense of the ancient Jewish Church.

First, in Isaiah 6:1ff. the prophet says, "*I saw the Lord sitting upon a throne, high and lifted up, and his train filled the temple. Above him stood the seraphim*[171] ... *And one called to another and said, 'Holy, holy, holy Lord of hosts, the whole earth is full of his glory'* ... *And the house was filled with smoke.*" That this house was the temple is expressly said at the end of the first verse. And the smoke was the sign of the *Shekinah* of God, with which the temple was now filled, as it was when he first entered into it (1Kg 8:10-11). In this way here, the Lord sitting upon his throne, was none other than God sitting upon his mercy-seat over the ark. That is, he was the Word of the Lord according to the opinion of the ancient Jewish Church, as has been abundantly proved before in this chapter. But this can also be seen here in their paraphrase; for whereas the prophet still speaking of the Lord whom he saw sitting on his throne (Isa 6:1), says, "*Then I heard the voice of the Lord, saying, 'Whom shall I send?*" (8), the Targum renders it, "*I heard the voice of the Word of the Lord, saying, 'Whom shall I send?'*" We Christians need not thank them for this, being fully assured, as we are by what the Apostle says in John 12:41 that this was none other than our Lord Jesus Christ. For there the Apostle, having quoted the words that Isaiah heard from the Lord that spoke to him (Isa 6:9-10) tells us, "*These things Isaiah said when he saw his glory, and spoke of him.*" That the

---

[171] Allix reads "cherubims."

Apostle here speaks of the Word made flesh, it is clear enough from the text. But besides, it has been proved by our writers beyond all contradiction.[172]

In the same way, that which the prophet Ezekiel saw was an appearance of God represented to him as a man sitting on a throne of glory (Ezek 1:26, 28; 10:1). The throne was upon wheels, after the manner of a *sella curulis*.[173] These were living wheels, animated and supported by cherubim (1:21), each of which had four faces (1:6) such as were carved on the walls of the temple (41:19). In short, even though he was in Chaldea (Babylon), that which Ezekiel saw was nothing other than the appearance of God still dwelling in his temple at Jerusalem. This, even though God was weary of it and was soon about to abandon it, to leave his dwelling place and allow it to be destroyed by the Chaldeans. To show that this was the meaning of it, he saw this glorious appearance of God, first, *"in his place"* (3:12), i.e. on the mercy-seat, in the temple (9:3).

Next, he saw him having left his place, gone to the *"threshold of the house."* Judges use to give judgment in the gate; so there, over the threshold of his house,

---

[172] See Plac. *Lib. ii. Disput.* 1. It should be noted that the Hebrew text does not talk about the "glory" or the shekinah in Isaiah 6. However, the Targum does. Thus, some scholars have argued that John is actually either targuming himself or was familiar with the old Targum on Isaiah 6:1 and is alluding to it. Either way, he is tapping into this ancient tradition, and this supports Allix's argument all the more.

[173] This refers to the Roman Emperor's "Chariot Seat," which basically represented political and military authority.

God pronounced sentence against his rebellious people (5-7). Afterwards, from the threshold of the house (10:4), the prophet saw the glory departing even farther. It *"mounted up from the earth over the midst of the city"* (10:18-19). Lastly, he saw it go from there and *"stand upon the mountain on the east side of the city"* (11:23), that is on the Mt. of Olives, which is before Jerusalem on the east (Zech 14:4), and so the Targum has it on this place.

After this departure of the Divine Presence, Ezekiel saw his forsaken temple and city destroyed and his people carried away into captivity (33:21ff.). After this he saw no more appearances of God until his people's return from his captivity; and then, the temple being rebuilt according to the measures given from God (chs. 40-42). The prophet could not but expect that God would return to it as of old. So, he saw it come to pass in his vision, *"Behold the glory of the God of Israel came from the way of the east* (where the prophet saw it last, at the Mt. of Olives, 43:2). So again, *"The glory of the Lord came into the house by the way of the gate whose prospect is toward the east"* (4). And, *"Behold the glory of the Lord filled the house"* (5). So again, *"It filled the house"* (44:4) now, as it had done in Solomon's time (1Kg 8:11).

All along in this prophecy of Ezekiel, there was but one Person who appeared, from the beginning to the end. In the beginning of this prophecy, it was God who appeared in his temple over the cherubim; and there we find him again at the end of this prophecy. But that it was none other but the Word who appeared in the temple, according to the sense of the ancient Jewish Church, has been proved so fully out of their Targums elsewhere, that we need not trouble ourselves about that any farther, though we cannot find it in the Targum on this book.[174]

In the books of Chronicles there is nothing remarkable of this kind, but except what has been considered already, in the account that we have given of the Divine appearances in the books of Kings. And there is no mention made of any such appearance in any of the other books that were written after the Babylonian captivity, except in the books of Daniel and Zechariah.[175] Of Daniel the Jews have not given us any Targum, therefore we have nothing to say of that book. They have given us a Targum, such as it is, of the book of Zechariah, which is the last we have to consider.

---

[174] The Memra does appear frequently in the Ezekiel Targum. A possible example that might have satisfied Allix could be, "... *by placing their threshold beside the threshold of My Holy Temple, and their buildings beside My Temple Court, with only a wall of My Holy Temple between My Memra and them. They defiled My holy name with their abominations which they committed, so I destroyed them. in My anger. Now let them put their idols and the corpses of their kings far away, so as not to sin before Me, and I will cause My Shekinah to dwell among them forever*" (Ezek 43:8-9).

[175] This again does not mean that the Memra is not to be found in these books. He appears quite often, but mostly in prophecy or in some kind of theological way. Allix is concerned with actual appearances.

In this book of Zechariah, we read of three angels who appeared to the prophet. The first appeared to him as a man (Zech 1:8, 10), but he is called an angel (9). In Zechariah's words, "*The angel who talked with me,*" is the title he is often given to distinguish him from all others in the same book (1:13, 14, 19; 2:3; 5:5, 6; 6:4). A second angel appeared to him also as "*a man*" with a measuring line in his hand (2:1). But whoever compares this text with Ezekiel 40:3-5 etc. will find that this, who appeared as "*a man,*" was truly an angel of God.

Next, the first angel going forth from the place where he appeared (Zech 2:3), "*another angel*" comes to meet him, and tells him, "*Run, speak to this young man*" (whether to the angel surveyor, or whether to Zechariah himself) and tell him, "*Jerusalem shall be inhabited*" etc. (2:4). He who commands another should be his superior. And yet this superior says that he himself was sent from God. But he said it in such terms that it showed he was God himself. This the reader will see more than once in his speech, which is continued from vs. 4 to the end of the chapter.

It appears especially in vv. 8, 9, and 11 of this chapter. First, in vs. 9. having declared what God would do for Jerusalem in these words, according to the Targum, "*The Lord has said, 'My Word shall be a wall of fire about her, and my Shekinah will I place in the midst of her.'*" He goes on to vs. 12, and there he delivers a message from God to his people in these words: "*Thus says the Lord of hosts (after the glory[176] which it was promised to bring upon you...).*" Here the sense is ambiguous; for it seems strange that the Lord of hosts should say another has sent me. But so it is again, and much more clearly expressed in vs. 13 where he says, "*Behold, I will shake my hand upon them, and they shall be spoil for those who served me.*" No one but God could say this, but he adds in the next words, "*And you shall know that the Lord of hosts has sent me,*" which plainly shows that though he styled himself God, yet he came as a Messenger from God.

This is plainer still when he says, "*Many nations shall be joined to the Lord in that day, and I [my Shekinah] will dwell in your midst*" (15). This again no one but God could say, and yet it follows, "*You (O Zion)[177] shall know that the Lord of hosts has sent me to you.*" Here we plainly see two persons called by the name of Jehovah; namely, one that sends, and another that is sent; so that this second Person is God, and yet he is also the Messenger of God.

So likewise, in the next chapter the angel that used to talk with the prophet showed him Joshua the high priest standing before the Angel of the Lord, and

---

[176] The note reads, "After the glory of his Shekinah being returned into the temple, when that was rebuilt, they should soon after see Babylon itself taken, and spoiled by their ancient servants the Persians."

[177] The original has a note that all of the pronouns are feminine and therefore refer to Zion.

Satan standing over against Joshua as his adversary (Zech 3:1). In vs. 2 the prophet hears the Lord say to Satan not once but twice, "*The Lord rebuke you,*" for he was maliciously bent against Joshua who has just come out of the captivity "*like a brand plucked out of the fire.*" He that was called the Angel (1) is now called the Lord (2), and this Lord intercedes with the Lord for his protecting Joshua against Satan. That which gave the Devil advantage against Joshua was his sins; which, as the Targum says, were the marriages of his sons to strange wives. Whatever his sins may have been, they are here called "*filthy garments;*" and Joshua is clothed in them before the angel (3-4). The angel commands all who stood about him, saying, "*Take away the filthy garments from him.*" Here again, by commanding the angels, he shows himself their superior. Afterwards, when the filthy garments are taken off, this Angel says to Joshua, "*Behold, I have caused your iniquity to pass from you;*" words, which, if a man had said them to another, the Jews would have accounted it blasphemy (Matt 9:2-3). "*For who* (say they) *can forgive sins but God alone?*"

But here was one who exercised that authority over the high priest himself. This could be none other than he who was called of God, a priest for ever after the order of Melchizedek (Ps 110:4), of whom the Jewish high priest, even Joshua himself, was but a figure. But he goes farther, adding, "*I will clothe you with pure vestments,*" that is, according to the Targum, "*I will clothe you with righteousness*" (5). And he said,[178] (again commanding the angels), "*Let them set a clean turban on his head; and they did so, and clothed him with garments, and the Angel of the Lord stood by.*" Here again he is called an Angel, at last, as he was at first (Zech 2:3). It is an angel's office to be the messenger of God; and so he often owned himself to be, in saying, "*The Lord sent me.*" And yet this Messenger of God commands the angels (2:4; 3:4-5) and himself stands by to see them do his commands (5).

This Angel calls Israel his people, and says, he will dwell among them (Zech 2:10-11). He takes it upon himself to protect his people (5), and to avenge them on their enemies (10). He intercedes with God (3:2). He forgives sin and confers righteousness (3:4). If all these things cannot be truly said of one and the same person, then here are two chapters together that are each of them half nonsense, and there is no way to reconcile them with sense, but by putting some kind of force upon the text, whether by changing the words, or by putting in other words, as Socinus honestly confesses he has done in his interpretation.[179] He says they must do it to make sense of the words. This is absolutely certain, since they only want to interpret the words as they see fit. But he and his followers

---

[178] The note reads *and he said*, Jon. Targ.
[179] Socin. in *Wick*. 1.ii. p. 565.

bring this necessity upon themselves. Those who feel compelled to set up new opinions must defend them with new Scriptures. For our part, we change nothing in the words; and in our way of understanding them we follow the judgment of the ancient Jewish Church which makes all these things perfectly agree to the *Logos*. This we see in Philo,[180] who often calls the *Logos* God; and yet as often calls him an angel, the messenger of God; and our high priest, and our mediator with God. The same has been shown of the Word elsewhere out of the Targums. And here in this Targum, though no doubt it has been carefully purged, yet by some oversight it is said that, *"The Word shall be a wall of fire about Jerusalem."* And if the modern Jews had not changed the third person into the first, it would have followed, that his Shekinah should be in the midst of her; as he himself says afterward (10-11), *"He would dwell in the midst of her;"* meaning in the temple, where the Word of God had his dwelling-place always before its destruction, as has been abundantly shown in this chapter, and as we showed from Ezekiel it was

---

[180] *On Dreams* 1.238-41; Eusebius, *Preparation for the Gospel* 7.15. *Deuteros Theos* [Second God]: Philo, *Questions on Genesis* 2.62. As Philo calls the Father, *protos theos* [First God]: *On the Migration of Abraham* 194. The Word as Angel: *The Heir of All Things* 205. Two Powers: *On Dreams* 162-63; *On the Unchangeableness of God* 109. Allix gives several more references, but we are unsure to which attribute these pertain. See *The Heir of All Things* 42.205; *De Somn.* p. 463. F. *De Prof.* p. 364. B; *De Prof.* 466. B; *De Somniss*, p. 594. E; *The Heir of All Things* 205; *Vit. Mos.* iii. P. 521. B.

promised he should dwell there again after its restoration.

Glossary of Works and Authors Cited

There are many obscure and long since forgotten authors and works cited in Allix's discussions on the Angel-Word. This Appendix contains a short biography of many of these men and some of those works. I have not included biographies of those sources in the section on Genesis 48:15-16.

ABARBANEL (1437-1508). Don Isaac Abravanel or Isaac ben Judah Arbanel. Portuguese Jewish statemen, religious Jew, scholar, Bible commentator and philosopher of the "Spanish Golden Age."

ABEN SUEB (15th cent.). Joel ibn Shu'aib. Spanish rabbi, preaching, commentator.

AKIBA (50-135). Akiva. A leading Jewish scholar and sage, a tanna of the latter part of the first century. He was a leading contributor to the Mishnah.

ALSHEK (1508-1593). Moshe Alshich. Prominent rabbi, preacher, commentator. Legend says his son was kidnapped as a child and became a Muslim and that a special prayer was written for his return.

AMBROSE OF MILAN (333–397). Bishop of Milan and teacher of Augustine who defended the divinity of the Holy Spirit and the perpetual virginity of Mary.

ARETHAS OF CAESAREA (c. 860–940). Byzantine scholar and disciple of Photius. He was a deacon in Constantinople, then archbishop of Caesarea from 901.

ARISTOBULUS OF ALEXANDRIA (181-124 B.C.). A Hellenistic Jewish philosopher, was the predecessor of Philo and tried to fuse Hebrew Scriptures with Greek thought.

ATHIAS. (16th cent.). Yom-Tov Ben Levi Athias or Jerónimo de Vargas, he produced and paid for a Spanish translation of the Bible called *The Ferrara Bible* (1553).

AUGUSTINE (354–430). Bishop of Hippo and a voluminous writer on philosophical, exegetical, theological and ecclesiological topics. In the West, he towers over all others.

AUTPERT AMBROSE (730-784). Frankish Benedictine monk who wrote commentaries on the Apocalypse, Psalms, and Song of Solomon.

BECHAI (1255-1340). Bahya ben Asher ibn Halawa. Distinguished Spanish rabbi who wrote a commentary on the Hebrew Bible.

BEDE THE VENERABLE (672–735). Born in Northumbria, at the age of seven he was put under the care of the Benedictine monks of Saints Peter and Paul at Jarrow and given a broad classical education in the monastic tradition.

BELLARMINE, ROBERT (1542 –1621). Italian Jesuit and Cardinal. He was an important figure in the Counter-Reformation and a proponent of the Council of Trent.

BERIT MENUCHAH is a work of practical Kabbalah written down in the 14th century by Rabbi Abraham ben Isaac of Granada. It contains a system of theurgy which uses secret names of God and his emanations for spiritual and magical purposes.

BUXTORF (1564-1629). Johannes Bustorf. Hebraist, professor of Hebrew at Basel (Switzerland), known as "Master of the Rabbis." (PA)

CLARK, SAMUEL (1626-1701). English Nonconformist, rector at Grendon Underwood, Buckinghamshire, and annotator of the Bible. He was a friend of John Owen, Richard Baxter, and George Whitefield.

Glossary

CLEMENT OF ALEXANDRIA (c. 150–215). A highly educated Christian convert from paganism, head of the catechetical school in Alexandria and pioneer of Christian scholarship.

CYPRIAN (200-258). Martyred bishop of Carthage who maintained that those baptized by schismatics and heretics had no share in the blessings of the church.

CYRIL OF ALEXANDRIA (375–444). Patriarch of Alexandria whose extensive exegesis and strong view of the unity of Christ led to the condemnation of Nestorius in 431.

DAVID THE LESS. Probably David ben Yom Tov ibn Bilia (c. 1300-1361). Portuguese Hebrew scholar, translator, philosopher, exegete, and poet who wrote *Me'or Enayim*, a commentary on the Pentateuch.

DRUSIUS (1550-1616). Johannes van den Driesche. Flemish Protestant divine, Orientalist, Christian Hebraist, and exegete.

ELIEZER (1st-2nd cent.). Eliezer ben Hurcanus, one of the most prominent sages of the 1st and 2nd centuries in Judea. He is the sixth most frequently mentioned sage in the Mishnah.

EUSEBIUS OF CAESAREA (c. 260/263–340). Bishop of Caesarea, partisan of the Emperor Constantine and first historian of the Christian church.

THE FERRARA BIBLE (1553). Made and paid for by Yom-Tov Ben Levi Athias (typographer) and Abraham ben Salomon Usque (translator) and dedicated to the Duke of Ferrara. It was a translation of an older circulating Spanish translation.

GEKATILIA, JOSEPH (1248-1305). Joseph ben Abraham Gikatilla. Spanish kabbalist.

GREGORY OF ELVIRA (fl. 359–385). Bishop of Elvira who wrote allegorical treatises in the style of Origen and defended the Nicene faith against the Arians.

GROTIUS, HUGO (1583-1645). Dutch Jurist and Arminian theologian, he is noted for his "governmental" or "moral government" theory of the atonement and for being imprisoned for his views.

HAYMO. At least three prominent Christians bear this name and Allix does not tell us which one he has in mind. These are Haymo of Halberstadt (d. 835) a German Benedictine monk, Haymo of Auxerre (d. 865) another German Benedictine, and Haymo of Faversham (d. 1243) an English Franciscan. The most likely candidate is Haymo of Halberstadt.

JAKULT (13th cent.). A collection of commentaries from various ancient books by **R. Shimeon of Frankfurt**.

JARKI (1040-1105). Shlomo Yitzchaki, also called Rashi, he was a medieval French rabbi and author of a commentary on the Tanakh.

JELAMMEDENU (8th cent.). A popular Homily-Midrash originating in Israel that bears **Tanchuma**'s name but was not written by him.

JEROME (c. 347–420). Gifted exegete and exponent of a classical Latin style, now best known as the translator of the Latin Vulgate. He defended the perpetual virginity of Mary, attacked Origen and Pelagius and supported extreme ascetic practices.

JOCHANAN (30-90 A.D.). R. Yohanan ben Zeccai. A primary contributor to the core text of the Mishnah.

JUSTIN MARTYR (100/110–165). Palestinian philosopher who was converted to Christianity. He traveled to Rome and wrote several apologies (defenses of the faith) against both pagans and Jews; he was eventually martyred.

KABBALAH. Esoteric method, discipline, and school of thought of Judaism. The **Zohar** (13th cent. but with oral tradition dating back to untold primordial time) is one of the main texts of Kabbalah.

KIRCHER, CONRAD (d. 1622). German philologian of Augsburg, Lutheran pastor first at Donauwerth and later at Jaxtdorf. He published a concordance of the LXX in 1607 called *Concordic veteris Testamenti Gracace Ebreis vocibus respondents*.

LEO THE GREAT (regn. 440–461). Bishop of Rome whose *Tome to Flavian* helped to strike a balance between Nestorian and Cyrilline positions at the Council of Chalcedon in 451.

LEVI BEN GERSOM (1288-1344). Best known as Gersonides or Magister Leo Hebraeus. French Jewish philosopher, Talmudist, Mathematician, physician, astronomer. Wrote several commentaries on Scripture.

LORINUS OF AVIGNON (1559-1634). Jesuit who published a commentary on Scripture.

Glossary 187

MAIMONIDES (1135-1204). Moses ben Maimon. Spanish born rabbi who become one of the most influential of all medieval Torah scholars.

MASIUS, ANDREAS (1514-73). Catholic priest, humanist, and one of the first Europeans to specialize in the Syriac language.

MENAHEM BEN BENJAMIN RECANATI (1223-1290). Italian rabbi who wrote a commentary on the Torah.

MENASSEH BEN ISRAEL (1604-1657). Manoel Dias Soeiro. Portuguese rabbi, kabbalist, writer, diplomat, and founded the first Hebrew printing press in Amsterdam in 1626. The book cited seems to be *Primo Questionum in Genesis*, previously published as *The Conciliator*.

MOSES BEN NAHMAN (1194-1270). Leading medieval Jewish scholar, rabbi, philosopher, physician, kabbalist, and biblical commentator. He lived most of his life in Girona, Catalonia (Spain).

MOSES BEN MAIMON. See **Maimonides**.

MUNSTERUS (1488-1552). Sebastian Münster. German cartographer, cosmographer, and Christian Hebraist scholar. Early on he was a Franciscan, then became Lutheran to accept a chair at the University of Basel.

NOVATIAN OF ROME (fl. 235–258). Roman theologian, otherwise orthodox, who formed a schismatic church after failing to become pope. His treatise on the Trinity states the classic Western doctrine.

ORIGEN (b. 185; fl. c. 200–254). Influential exegete and systematic theologian from Alexandria, Egypt. He was condemned (perhaps unfairly) for maintaining the preexistence of souls while purportedly denying the resurrection of the body. His extensive works of exegesis focus on the spiritual meaning of the text.

PHILO (20 BC – 50 AD). Alexandrians Jewish Hellenistic philosopher who lived during the time of Christ, he is one of the best monotheistic proponents who believed in a "second God" called the Logos, which lends itself nicely towards an understanding of Christ in the OT.

PROCOPIUS OF GAZA (c. 465–c. 530). A Christian exegete educated in Alexandria. He wrote numerous theological works and commentaries on Scripture (particularly the Hebrew Bible), the latter marked by the allegorical exegesis for which the Alexandrian school was known.

REUCHLIN, JOHANN (1455-1522). German humanist and Greek and Hebrew scholar. He wrote a treatise *On the Art of Kabbalah* (1517).

Rupertus. Allix probably has in mind Rupert of Deutz (1075-1129) an influential Benedictine from Belgium.

Sanctius (1553-1628). Gaspar Sanchez. Spanish Jesuit. Taught at Oropesa in Madrid. Spent thirteen years writing commentaries on Scripture.

Samuel (165-254). Samuel of Nehardea or Samuel bar Abba. One of the early rabbinical authorities cited in Genesis Rabbah.

Serrano, Joseph Franco (1652-1695). Rabbi, teacher of Hebrew at the Portuguese synagogue in Amsterdam. He provided a Spanish translation of the books of Moses with marginal notes from the Talmud and the Rabbis who commented on them.

Shimeon of Frankfurt (13th cent.). Rabbi who wrote the **Jalkut**.

Socinianism. Named for Italian theologian Fausto Sozzini (Lat: **Faustus Socinus**). It is nontrinitarian in its view of Christ and precursor to many forms of Unitarianism within Protestantism.

Socinus, (Faustus 1539-1604). Fausto Paolo Sozzini. Italian theologian and founder of Socinianism, precursor to many forms of Unitarianism within Protestantism.

Solomon ben Melek (16th cent.) From Fez, Morocco. He published his Bible commentary *Michlol Jophi (Perfection of Beauty)* in 1549 through a press in Constantinople.

Strabo, Walafrid (808-849). Alemannic Benedictine monk and theological writer who lived in southern Germany. He wrote on the Psalms and Leviticus.

Tanchuma (350-71). Tanchuma bar Abba. Jewish Rabbi of the 5th generation amora (Jewish scholars of the period from 200-500 AD).

Targum. A Targum is a paraphrastic rendition of the Hebrew Scripture into Aramaic for Jews who did not speak Hebrew. They contain both oral tradition and interpretation of the Scripture and were probably first written down around the first century by the Jews.

Tertullian (c. 155/160–225/250). Carthaginian apologist and polemicist who laid the foundations of Christology and Trinitarian Orthodoxy in the West, though he himself was later estranged from the catholic tradition.

THEODORET OF CYR (c. 393–466). Bishop of Cyr (Cyrrhus), he was an opponent of Cyril who commented extensively on Old Testament texts as a lucid exponent of Antiochene exegesis.

USQUE, ABRAHAM (16th cent.). Also known as Duarte Pinel (Pinhel). Marrano printer. Born in Portugal but fled from the Inquisition shortly after 1543, established himself at Ferrara, and became associated with the press established by the Spanish ex-Marrano, **Yom-Tov ben Levi Athias** (Jerónimo de Vargas). He followed Athias' plan of publishing Jewish liturgies in the vernacular, as well as other texts intended to facilitate the Marranos' return to Judaism. Usque's name first appears in connection with the famous Bible translation of 1553, the so-called *Ferrara Bible*.

VECHNER, DANIEL (1572-1632). Taught at the Gymnasium at Goldberg (Germany). Wrote several works in Latin. (PÁ)

VICTORINUS OF PETOVIUM (d. c. 304). Latin biblical exegete. With multiple works attributed to him, his sole surviving work is the *Commentary on the Apocalypse* and perhaps some fragments from *Commentary on Matthew*. a spiritual disciple of Origen. Victorinus died during the first year of Diocletian's persecution, probably in 304.

Zohar (13th cent.). The foundational text of Kabbalah. It first appeared in Spain in the 13th century and was published by Moses de León who ascribed it to Shimon bar Yochai (Rashbi), a rabbi of the 2nd century.

Author Index

A

Abenezra 119
Abraham ben Salomon Usque 16
Abravanel, Don Isaac 26, 30
Ainsworth, Henry 60
Akiba 141
Alshich, Moshe 26
Ambrose 49
Apostolic Constitutions 22
Aquila a Jew ... 91
Aquinas, Thomas 49
Arethas of Caesarea 49
Aristobulus 92
Athanasius 57
Augustine 46
Autpert Ambrose 49

B

Bahya ben Asher ibn Halawa. 34
Barker, Margaret 7
Bauckham, Richard 7
Bavinck, Herman 73
Bede 49
Bellarmine, Robert 38
Bomberg, Daniel 123
Boyarin, Daniel 7
Boyce, James P. 70
Buxtorf, Johannes ... 43, 120

C

Cælius of Pannonia 49
Calvin, John 59
Chrysostom, John 22, 58
Clark, Samuel 144
Clarkson, David 64
Clement of Alexandria . 22, 23
Clifford, Hywel 4
Cyprian 22
Council of Sirmium 22

Cyril 22, 46

D

Dabney, R. L.. 69
David ben Yom Tov ibn Bilia 35
De Gols, Gerard 90
Diodati, Giovani 60
Dionysius the Areopagite . 24
Drusius 91
see Abraham ben Salonom 16

E

Eusebius .. 22, 92, 121

F

Fossum, Jarl E. 8
Frame, John ... 75

G

Gathercole, Simon 8
Gill, John 67
Gregory of Elvira 23

Grotius, Hugo 14, 92, 112, 124

H

Hannah, Darrell D. 8
Haymo of Halberstadt 49
Heiser, Michael S. 8
Henry, Matthew 66
Hodge, A. A. 69
Hughes, George 61
Hurtado, Larry W. 8
Hyde, Edward 62

J

Jerome 17, 44, 91
Joel ibn Shu'aib 35
Johannes van den Driesche 16
Joseph b. Abraham Gikatilla ... 124
Joseph ben Abraham Gikatilla 35
Josephus 131
Justin Martyr . 22, 23, 46, 78, 79

K

Kelly, Douglas 76
Kircher, Conrad 17

L

Lee, Aquila H. I. 8
Leo 23
Lorinus of Avignon 24
Luther, Martin 58

M

Maimonides ... 31, 37, 157
Manasseh ben Israel 54
Manoel Dias Soeiro 35
Masius 162
Masius, Andreas 39
Menahem ben Benjamin Recanati 23
Metatron . 42, 43, 44
Metzger, Bruce M. 3
Moses ben Maimon 37
Moses ben Nahman 33, 55, 162
Münster, Sebastian 26

N

Neusner, Jacob 21
Novatian ... 23, 56

O

Origen 22
Owen, John 63

P

Packer, J. I. 75
Perkins, William 59
Philo 23, 32, 100, 101, 106, 111, 112, 113, 115, 116, 119, 120, 125, 126, 131, 134, 135, 147, 156, 181

Poole, Matthew 65
Procopius of Gaza 23

R

R. Eliezer 45
R. Gekatalia 35
R. Johanan 21
R. Levi ben Gersom 36
R. Menachem de Rekanah 41
R. Menachem of Rekan ... 34, 55
R. Menasseh ... 36
R. Moses Ben Nachman 55
R. Nehunia ben Acana 53
R. Shimeon of Frankfurt 28
R. Solomon 33
R. Yohanan ben Zeccai 27
Reuchlin, Johann 44
Reymond, Robert 74
Ridgley, Thomas 67
Rodkinson, Michael L. ... 21
Rupert of Deutz 49

S

Sanchez, Gaspar 24
Schmid, Heinrich 67
Segal, Alan F. ... 8
Serrano, Joseph Franco 30
Socinus 180
Solomon ben Melek 20

Author Index

Sproul, R. C. 76
Strong Augustus 71
Stuckenbruck, Loren T. 8

T

Tanchuma bar Abba 33
Tertullian . 22, 46
Theodoret of Cyrus 23
Turretin, Francis 64

U

Usquez .... *See* Abraham ben Salonon Usque

V

Vechner, Daniel 112
Victorinus of Pettau 49
Vos, Geerhardus 74
Vreugdenhil, Arjen 24

W

Walafrid Strabo 49
Warfield, B. B. 72
Witsius, Herman 65

Y

Yitzchaki, Shlomo 44
Yom-Tov Ben Levi Athias 16

Z

Zohar 33, 52

Scripture Index

Genesis

Gen 1..............99
Gen 1:26..71, 80, 101
Gen 1:27........128
Gen 1:28........128
Gen 3:8..........129
Gen 3:9..........129
Gen 3:10........129
Gen 3:22.........71
Gen 5:22..........20
Gen 11:7..........71
Gen 15:6......2, 32
Gen 16:2–13 ...72
Gen 16:6–13 ..72, 75
Gen 16:7..68, 73, 133
Gen 16:7–13 ...74
Gen 16:9........133
Gen 16:9, 13 ...71
Gen 16:10......68, 133
Gen 16:10, 11. 73
Gen 16:11........68
Gen 16:13 68, 70, 73, 133
Gen 16:13;......70
Gen 18............72
Gen 18:1........126
Gen 18:1, 14, 17 68
Gen 18:1, 17, 20, 26, 33 70
Gen 18:1–33 ...74
Gen 18:2, 17 ...69
Gen 18:3..........73

Gen 18:14, 18 .73
Gen 18:15-16 137
Gen 19 72
Gen 19:1 68
Gen 19:24.....123
Gen 20...........133
Gen 20:13 71
Gen 21:1 68
Gen 21:11 68
Gen 21:13 68
Gen 21:14 68
Gen 21:16 134
Gen 21:17 68
Gen 21:17–20 72, 75
Gen 21:18 68, 73, 134
Gen 22 72
Gen 22:2 131
Gen 22:11, 15 .73
Gen 22:11, 16 .71
Gen 22:11–12 .75
Gen 22:11-16 ..72
Gen 22:11–18 .74
Gen 22:12 73
Gen 24:7, 40 ..73, 74
Gen 24:7; 40 ...72
Gen 26:2 134
Gen 26:3 134
Gen 26:24....134, 135
Gen 28:10–17 .74
Gen 28:11-22 ..76
Gen 28:11–22 .68
Gen 28:13 ......69, 135
Gen 28:13-16 135

Gen 28:13–17. 72
Gen 28:13–22. 70
Gen 28:15, 20, 21 65
Gen 28:20-21. 28
Gen 31:11 68, 73, 136
Gen 31:11, 13. 69
Gen 31:11 13 71, 72, 76
Gen 31:11–13. 72
Gen 31:11–13. 74
Gen 31:11–13. 74
Gen 31:11–13. 75
Gen 31:13 70, 73, 136
Gen 32:9 70
Gen 32:9, 10, 11. 29
Gen 32:9, 31... 69
Gen 32:9-11 ... 65
Gen 32:22-32. 76
Gen 32:24, 28, 30 76
Gen 32:24–30 72, 74
Gen 32:24ff.... 73
Gen 32:25 68
Gen 32:26 63
Gen 32:28, 30. 73
Gen 32:29 90
Gen 32:30 70, 75
Gen 35:3 65
Gen 35:7 71
Gen 35:9 ..... 128, 135, 136
Gen 37:7-15 ... 76

Gen 48:3-4 .... 19, 135
Gen 48:15 . 20, 41
Gen 48:15-16 .. 4, 6, 15, 64, 68, 69, 70, 71, 72, 73, 74, 75, 76, 89
Gen 48:16 29, 33, 34, 38, 40, 51, 59, 61, 62, 63, 65, 67, 73, 76, 89
Gen 49 29
Gen 49:24 41
Gen 49:25 . 30, 35

Exodus

Ex 3 .... 43, 119
Ex 3:1 171
Ex 3:2 69, 70, 139
Ex 3:2, 6 70
Ex 3:2-3 161
Ex 3:2-5 72
Ex 3:2–6 74
Ex 3:2f 72, 73
Ex 3:4 139
Ex 3:4, 6 70
Ex 3:4, 7 70
Ex 3:6 ... 139, 171
Ex 3:8 73
Ex 3:14, 15 69
Ex 3:16 139
Ex 13:21... 69, 70, 72, 74, 119, 147
Ex 14:19... 35, 69, 70, 72, 73, 74, 119, 147
Ex 14:24.. 69, 147
Ex 15:3 86
Ex 15:3, 11 90
Ex 15:11 90
Ex 15:25 147
Ex 16:7, 10 ... 148
Ex 17:14 148
Ex 17:15 148
Ex 17:8ff. 148
Ex 20:1, 2 69
Ex 23 .... 44, 127
Ex 23:20... 59, 64, 65, 69, 73
Ex 23:20-21 ... 59, 64
Ex 23:20–23 ... 72, 73, 74
Ex 23:21 73
Ex 23:31 87
Ex 24 127
Ex 24:19 52
Ex 25:21 69
Ex 25:40 150
Ex 27:31 150
Ex 27:33 150
Ex 32:34 .... 72, 74
Ex 32:34; 69
Ex 32:34–33:5 . 74
Ex 33 33
Ex 33:10 147
Ex 33:14 74
Ex 33:14f 72
Ex 33:2f 72
Ex 37:9 151

Leviticus

Lev 7:15 167

Numbers

Num 6:22ff 38
Num 6:24, 26 .. 72
Num 7:89 141
Num 10:35 ... 119
Num 12:5 147
Num 14 127
Num 20:16 72
Num 22:22 69
Num 22:22–35 74
Num 22:35 ... 158
Num 32–35 69

Deuteronomy

Dt 4:33, 36, 39 69
Dt 12:5, 11 ... 169
Dt 32:9 85
Dt 32:48-49 .. 156
Dt 33:1 156
Dt 34:1 156

Joshua

Josh 5:13 .. 69, 70, 163
Josh 5:13, 14 ... 72
Josh 5:13-14 . 160
Josh 5:13-15 ... 84
Josh 5:13–15.... 74
Josh 5:14 160
Josh 5:15 161
Josh 6:2 .... 69, 70, 161

Judges

Jdg 2:1–4 69
Jdg 2:1–5 74
Jdg 6:11-12 ... 162
Jdg 6:11-22 69
Jdg 6:11–23 74
Jdg 6:11–24.... 72, 74
Jdg 6:14 162
Jdg 6:15 119
Jdg 6:16 162
Jdg 6:20-22 ... 162
Jdg 6:21 73
Jdg 6:23-25 ... 162
Jdg 6:27 162
Jdg 7:18, 20 ... 163
Jdg 9:13–23 75
Jdg 13 163
Jdg 13:2–23 72
Jdg 13:3 ..... 69, 73
Jdg 13:3–22 74
Jdg 13:18 90
Jdg 13:20–22 ... 72
Jdg 13:21-22 ... 69

Ruth

Ruth 4:8 17

1 Samuel

1Sa 3:21 163, 164
1Sa 3:3-4 163

Scripture Index

1Sa 8:16..........87

2 Samuel

2Sa 6:18..........87
2Sa 24:14.......166
2Sa 24:15.......164
2Sa 24:16 74, 165
2Sa 24:16-17 165
2Sa 24:17.......165

1 Kings

1Kg 3:5..........167
1Kg 3:15.......167
1Kg 8:6..........169
1Kg 8:10-11 169, 173
1Kg 8:11.......175
1Kg 8:12-61.169
1Kg 8:15.......166
1Kg 9:1..........169
1Kg 9:2.167, 169
1Kg 9:3..........169
1Kg 19..........170
1Kg 19:5, 7...172
1Kg 19:8.......171
1Kg 19:13.....171
1Kg 22:19-23 .90
1Kg 22:19ff. .172

2 Kings

2Kg 1.............172
2Kg 19:34.....166
2Kg 19:35.....172
2Kg 20:6.......166

1 Chronicles

1Ch 7:12........169
1Ch 21:13.....164
1Ch 21:16.....165

2 Chronicles

2Ch 1:2-4.....168
2Ch 1:6..........168
2Ch 1:7..........168
2Ch 6:4..........170

1Co 10:4, 9.....64

1Co 10:9.........59
1Co 6:2...........95
1Jn 1:1.............69
1Jn 1:1, 5 137
1Jn 5:7............78
1Pe 3:20........129

Nehemiah

Neh 9:7–28 69

Job

Job 19:25 ....2, 64

Psalms

Ps 2 83
Ps 19:14 29
Ps 23:1 101
Ps 33:6......81, 93
Ps 34:19 29
Ps 34:7 69
Ps 35:5 69
Ps 45:6, 7 71
Ps 68 151
Ps 72. 90
Ps 77:14 90
Ps 105:1 71
Ps 110 83
Ps 110:1 95
Ps 110:4 179

Proverbs

Prov 3 83
Prov 8 72
Prov 8:22 83
Prov 8:22 92
Prov 8:25 83
Prov 30:4 2

Isaiah

Isa 6:1 173
Isa 6:1ff..........173
Isa 6:3........64, 72
Isa 6:8......71, 173
Isa 6:9-10......173
Isa 9:6......57, 163
Isa 9:7 90
Isa 11:2-3 48

Isa 23:14......... 29
Isa 43:14......... 64
Isa 47:4..... 29, 64
Isa 59:20... 62, 64
Isa 63:7, 9 69
Isa 63:8... 73, 163
Isa 63:8, 9 72
Isa 63:8-10...... 32
Isa 63:8-9....... 73
Isa 63:9.... 42, 67, 69, 75, 90
Isa 63:16......... 29

Ezekiel

Ezek 1:6....... 174
Ezek 1:21..... 174
Ezek 1:24 44
Ezek 1:26, 28 174
Ezek 3:12 174
Ezek 9:3 174
Ezek 9:5-7.... 175
Ezek 10:1 174
Ezek 10:4 175
Ezek 10:18-19 175
Ezek 11:23 ... 175
Ezek 33:21ff. 175
Ezek 40:3-5.. 177
Ezek 41:19 ... 174
Ezek 42-43... 175
Ezek 43:2 175
Ezek 43:4 175
Ezek 43:5 175
Ezek 44:4 175

Daniel

Dan 3:25 91
Dan 4:17 90
Dan 7:8 48
Dan 7:9ff........ 90

Hosea

Hos 12:2, 5..... 69
Hos 12:3-4... 137
Hos 12:4.. 62, 72, 73, 74
Hos 12:4, 5..... 76

Hos 12:4–6 68

Zechariah

Zech 1:12–15 .. 69
Zech 1:13-14 177
Zech 1:19 177
Zech 1:8, 10 . 177
Zech 1:8–12:3 . 73
Zech 1:9 177
Zech 12:8 74
Zech 14:4 175
Zech 2:1 177
Zech 2:10 180
Zech 2:10-11
 .... 180, 181
Zech 2:11 177
Zech 2:3 177, 180
Zech 2:4 177, 180
Zech 2:5 180
Zech 2:8-9 177
Zech 3:1 179
Zech 3:2 . 69, 179, 180
Zech 3:3-4 179
Zech 3:4 180
Zech 3:4-5 180
Zech 3:9 46
Zech 5:1 69
Zech 5:5-6 177
Zech 6:15 69
Zech 6:4 177

Malachi

Mal 2:7 67
Mal 3:1 .... 42, 59, 64, 67, 73, 74, 75

Matthew

Matt 1:21 65
Matt 11:10 67
Matt 9:2-3 179

Mark

Mark 1:2 67

Luke

Luke 7:27 67

John

John 1:18 69
John 5:36 69
John 6:46 69
John 10 42
John 12:41 173

Acts

Acts 7:31 24
Acts 7:30–35 ... 69
Acts 7:38 69
Acts 10:25-26 .. 60

Romans

Rom 4:22 130
Rom 4:9 130
Rom 10:14 60

1 Corinthians

1Co 10:4 40

Galatians

Gal 1:1 47
Gal 3:6 130

Ephesians

Eph 1:2 39
Eph 5:5 47

Colossians

Col 2:18 46

1 Timothy

2Ti 4:18 66

2 Peter

2Pe 2:16 158

Hebrews

Heb 1:3 82
Heb 4:12 86
Hos 1:7 71

James

Jam 2:23 130

Jude

Jude 5 2

Revelation

Rev 1:4 ...... 45, 47
Rev 1:20 67
Rev 3:1 47
Rev 4:8 47
Rev 5:6 48
Rev 19:10 . 60, 75, 160
Rev 22:8 60
Rev 22:9 .. 75, 160

Targums

TGen 1 107
TGen 1:1 105
TGen 1:27 105
TGen 2:8 105
TGen 3:8-10 105
TGen 5:24 105
TGen 6:7 102
TGen 7:16 ... 106, 129
TGen 8:21 ... 102, 130
TGen 11:8 106
TGen 12:17 .. 106
T1Ch 13:6 120
TGen 15:1 ... 106, 130
TGen 15:5 130
TGen 15:6 ... 102, 130
TGen 15:7 ... 102, 130
TGen 15:9 102
TGen 15:9ff. 130
TGen 15:13 .. 102
TGen 16:13 .. 133
TGen 18:2 .. 106

Scripture Index

TGen 19:24..106
TGen 21:20.102, 134
TGen 21:23..102
TGen 21:33..106
TGen 22:8...106, 132
TGen 22:14.106, 135
TGen 22:16-17 132
TGen 24:33..106
TGen 26:24, 28 106
TGen 27:28..135
TGen 28:20..136
TGen 28:20-21 136
TGen 30:22..106
TGen 31:3.....106
TGen 31:5.....135
TGen 35:9...131, 136
TGen 38:25..107
TGen 39:2-3 102
TGen 46:4....107
TGen 48:10..135
TGen 49:25.107, 131
TGen 50:20..107

TEx 1:21 107
TEx 2:5 107
TEx 3 107
TEx 3:12 103
TEx 3:14 116
TEx 3:14-15.118
TEx 4:12 .....103, 107
TEx 6:4 118
TEx 6:8107, 130, 133, 134
TEx 12:29 ...107, 142
TEx 12:42 ...108, 116
TEx 12:43 130

TEx 13:8......108, 142
TEx 13:17.....108
TEx 13:18.....143
TEx 14:15.....143
TEx 14:22.....143
TEx 14:24....143, 147
TEx 14:24, 31 108
TEx 14:25.....143
TEx 14:32.....103
TEx 15:2.......103
TEx 15:8......108, 143
TEx 15:10.....143
TEx 15:25....108, 144
TEx 16:8......103, 148
TEx 17:1ff....148
TEx 18:19.....103
TEx 19:17....103, 144
TEx 19:3.......144
TEx 19:5.......108
TEx 19:8.......144
TEx 19:9......108, 144
TEx 20:1.......108
TEx 20:1ff....145
TEx 20:19.....145
TEx 20:24.....149
TEx 23:20-22 108
TEx 25:22....141, 149, 151
TEx 29:42....103, 149
TEx 30:6.......103, 149, 151
TEx 30:36.....103, 141
TEx 31:13, 17 103
TEx 32:13.....134
TEx 32:35.....153

TEx 33:9...... 147
TEx 33:9, 11 108
TEx 33:19.... 108
TEx 33:22.... 103
TEx 33:23.... 108
TEx 33:35.... 108
TEx 34:5...... 108

TLev 1 108
TLev 8:35 103
TLev 18:30.. 103
TLev 22:9.... 103
TLev 23:11.. 109
TLev 26:11.. 104
TLev 26:46.. 150

TNum 7:89. 141, 151
TNum 9:19.. 103
TNum 9:19, 23 109
TNum 9:8.... 109
TNum10:35. 151
TNum 10:35-36 .... 109, 120
TNum 10:36 152
TNum 11:20104, 153
TNum 11:35, 36 118
TNum 12:6.. 109
TNum 14:9.. 104
TNum 14:11 104
TNum 14:20109, 154
TNum 14:30 133
TNum 14:41 153
TNum 20:12 104
TNum 20:24103, 104
TNum 21:6.. 153
TNum 21:6-9 109
TNum 22:9.. 157
TNum 22:18 109
TNum 22:20 157
TNum 22:22 157

TNum 22:31 104
TNum 23 104
TNum 23:4, 16
.... 158
TNum 23:8, 21
.... 152
TNum 25:4. 109, 154
TNum 27:16 155

TDt 1:1 109, 143
TDt 1:10 109
TDt 1:26 153
TDt 1:30 104
TDt 1:30, 32 109
TDt 1:32-33 104, 143, 147
TDt 3:2 109, 153
TDt 3:21-22. 155
TDt 3:22 104
TDt 4:3 109
TDt 4:7 110, 118
TDt 4:12 110
TDt 4:23-25. 110
TDt 4:24 152
TDt 4:33 ..... 110, 145
TDt 4:33, 36 104
TDt 4:34 109
TDt 4:36 145
TDt 5 110
TDt 5:5 104, 145
TDt 5:23 146
TDt 6:13 110
TDt 6:22 109
TDt 8:2-3 104
TDt 9:3 153
TDt 9:23 153
TDt 11:23 110
TDt 12:5 149
TDt 12:5, 11 169
TDt 13:19 104
TDt 15:5 104
TDt 18:16 146
TDt 20:1 ..... 104, 142
TDt 21:5 110

TDt 24:18 142
TDt 24:19 152
TDt 26:5 ..... 110, 133
TDt 26:14 104
TDt 26:17 150
TDt 26:18 ... 110, 150
TDt 28 142
TDt 28:1-2 ... 104
TDt 28:15 104
TDt 28:20ff.. 154
TDt 28:45 104
TDt 28:62 104
TDt 28:63 152
TDt 29:1-2 .. 142
TDt 29:22 110
TDt 30:20 104
TDt 30:3 154
TDt 30:8, 10 104
TDt 30:9 152
TDt 31:2-3 .. 155
TDt 31:4 155
TDt 31:5 155
TDt 31:6 155
TDt 31:6, 8 .. 104
TDt 31:7 ..... 110, 133
TDt 31:7-8... 156
TDt 31:23 156
TDt 32:36 ... 110, 154
TDt 32:39...... 47, 110
TDt 32:49 110
TDt 33:27 104
TDt 33:3 104
TDt 34:1 110
TDt 34:10 141
TDt 34:10-11
.... 118
TDt 34:11 142
TDt 34:4 110
TDt 34:5 156
TDt 34:5-12. 110
TDt 34:6 ..... 117, 131

TDt 34:9........157

TJosh 10:14..161
TJosh 23:3 161
TJosh 23:10..161
TJosh 23:13 ..162

TJdg 6:12-13 163
TJdg 6:16......162

T2Sam 6:2 120

T1Kg 9 170
T1Kg 9:7 167
T1Kg 19:11-12
.................117

T1Ch 29:11 ..117

T2Chr 32:21 117

TPs 110:5 180
TPs 68:11, 18
.................117

TIsa 6:1ff. 172

TEzek 43:8-9 176

TZech 2:12 ...177
TZech 2:13 ...178
TZech 2:15 ...178
TZech 2:9 177

Apocrypha

1Esd 1:50-51 ..88
1Esd 1:28 93
1Esd 1:47 93
1Esd 1:57 93
1Esd 2:5 87

2Ma 1:25 88
2Ma 11:6 95
2Ma 14:35 88
2Ma 15:22-23 .95
2Ma 15:34, 27.96

Scripture Index

2Ma 2:17 88
2Mac 11:6 89

Bar 3:37 95

EpJer 6, 7 89

Est 13:15 85
Est 13:15-17 ... 85

Jdt 16:13-14 ... 81
Jdt 16:14 93
Jdt 5:18 87
Jdt 9:7 86
Jdt 9:8 .... 87, 88

PrAz 36 88

Sir 1:4 .... 91, 93
Sir 17:17 89
Sir 24:18 ... 83, 92
Sir 24:23 84
Sir 24:3 82
Sir 24:4 83
Sir 24:8 84
Sir 24:9 91
Sir 39:8 94
Sir 45:5 84
Sir 46:5-6 84
Sir 48:24 94
Sir 48:3-5 85
Sir 51:10 ... 83, 94

Tob 5:16 88
Tob 8:6 81

Wis 1:4-7 94
Wis 16:12 86
Wis 16:8, 12 ... 31
Wis 18:15-16 84, 86
Wis 19:9 83
Wis 3:8 95
Wis 7:22 83
Wis 7:25 82
Wis 9:1 .... 81, 83
Wis 9:17 .. 81, 94
Wis 9:4 81
Wis 18:15 92

Pseudepigripha

TLevi 5:5-6 51

ABOUT THE EDITOR

Doug has pastored the Reformed Baptist Church of Northern Colorado since 2001. He graduated from Bethel College in 1992, majoring in Marketing and minoring in Bible. He was a youth pastor for four years in Denver. He holds the Master of Divinity degree from Denver Seminary (2001).

Doug has served on councils and boards for two Baptist Associations, the current one which he helped found in 2016. The Reformed Baptist Network seeks to glorify God through fellowship and cooperation in fulfilling the Great Commission to the ends of the earth. There are currently 42 churches in this international association of churches.

Doug has co-hosted the radio show Journey's End, the Peeranormal podcast, started the Waters of Creation Publishing Company, owned two small business in Minneapolis, and has appeared on numerous podcasts and radio shows.

Married since 1994, he and Janelle are the proud parents of four beautiful young girls. Born and raised in Colorado, he has climbed all 54 of Colorado's 14,000 ft. mountains and also Mt. Rainier (WA) and Mt. Shasta (CA).

To find out more about any of these things go to:
https://www.dougvandorn.com/

The Church website is
https://rbcnc.com

Books in the Christ In All Scripture Series

John Owen's treatment is perfect for those wanting to ground their theology of the Angel in the high orthodoxy of the Reformation. The quotations from the Fathers bolster his thesis.

Peter Allix's work is comprehensive and is especially helpful for those familiar with modern scholarship wishing to root their theology in conservative Protestant/Reformed orthodoxy.

Gerard De Gols' study, especially the second half, is imminently practical and would help anyone wanting to learn more about why it matters that Christ is present in the Old Testament.

Owen, Allix, and De Gols together in one volume, minus quotations from the Fathers and Reformers.

The Second Edition of *From the Shadows to the Savior*, it explores even more of the titles given to Christ in the OT than Allix goes into.

Practical sermons are for the further exploration of the fullness of Christ, especially as he is found in the NT.

Other Books by Doug Van Dorn

Giants: Sons of the Gods
The bestselling non-fiction book on Genesis 6 and the Nephilim.
150 reviews. 4.5+++ stars on Amazon.

Goliath. You know the story. But why is it in the Bible? Is it just to give us a little moral pick-me-up as we seek to emulate a small shepherd boy who defeated a giant? Have you ever wondered where Goliath came from? Did you know he had brothers, one with 24 fingers and toes? Did you know their ancestry is steeped in unimaginable horror? Genesis 6. The Nephilim. The first few verses of this chapter have long been the speculation of supernatural events that produced demigods and a flood that God used to destroy the whole world. The whole world remembers them. Once upon a time, all Christians knew them. But for many centuries this view was mocked, though it was the only known view at the time of the writing of the New Testament. Today, it is making a resurgence among Bible-believing scholars, and for good reason. The Nephilim were on the earth in those days, and also afterward...

    This book delves deep into the dark and ancient recesses of our past to bring you rich treasures long buried. It is a carefully researched, heavily footnoted, and selectively illustrated story of the giants of the Bible. There is more here than meets the eye, much more. Here you will learn the invisible, supernatural storyline of the Bible that is always just beneath the surface, lurking like the spawn of the ancient leviathan. It is a storyline no person can afford to ignore any longer. Unlike other more sensational books on the topic, there is no undue speculation to be found here. The author is a Bible-believing Christian who refuses to use such ideas to tell you the end of the world is drawing nigh. Once you discover the truth about these fantastic creatures, you will come to see the ministry and work of Jesus Christ in a very new and exalting light. Come. Learn the fascinating, sobering, yet true story of real giants who played a significant role in the bible … and still do so today.

Available in Paperback or Kindle at Amazon.com

The Unseen Realm: Q & A Companion
Edited by Michael Heiser.
Published by Lexham Press.

In *The Unseen Realm*, Dr. Michael S. Heiser unpacked 15 years of research while exploring what the Bible really says about the supernatural world. That book has nearly 900 reviews and a five-star rating. It is a game-changer

Doug helps you further explore *The Unseen Realm* with a fresh perspective and an easy-to-follow format. The book summarizes key concepts and themes from Heiser's book and includes questions aimed at helping you gain a deeper understanding of the biblical author's supernatural worldview.

The format is that of a catechism: A Question followed by the Answer. There are 95 Questions (nod to Martin Luther) divided into 12 Parts:

Part I—God
Part II—The Lesser Gods
Part III—The Sons of God
Part IV—Divine Council
Part V—Sin, Rebellion, and the Fall
Part VI—Rebellion before the flood
Part VII—Rebellion after the flood
Part VIII—The Promise Anticipated
Part IX—The Promise Fulfilled
Part X—The Good News

Available in Paperback or Kindle at Amazon.com or on the Bible-software platform Logos at Logos.com

From the Shadows to the Savior:
Christ in the Old Testament

Few subjects are as important--yet ignored or misapplied--as the one addressed in this book. Jesus Christ is the absolute center and focus of the totality of God's word. Many people confess this belief, since Jesus himself taught it (Luke 24:27; John 5:39). Christians have done well to see this on one or two levels, yet truly understanding just how primary he is as an actor—even in the Old Testament—is something few have considered.

In this book, adapted from a series of blog posts for the Decablog, Doug helps us see the light of Christ that emerges from the dark hallways of Scriptures that so many find outdated, unintelligible, and irrelevant for today's Church.

Learn how Christ is found in such things as prophecy, typology, and the law. Then, come in for a deeper study of how the Person himself is actually present, walking, speaking, and acting, beginning in the very first book of the Bible. Learn how words such as "Word," "Name," "Glory," and "Wisdom" are all ideas that the Scripture itself attaches to Christ who in the OT is called The Angel of the LORD. Then see if such ideas don't radically change the way you think about all of God's word in this truly life-changing summary of Christ in the Old Testament.

Chapters:
NT Passages and Reflections
Christ in Prophecy
Christ in Typology
Christ and the Law
Christ: The Angel of the LORD
Christ: The Word of God
Christ: The Name of the LORD
Christ: The Wisdom of God
Christ: The Son of God
Christ: The Glory of God
Christ: The Right Arm of God

Available in Paperback or Kindle at Amazon.com

Waters of Creation:
A Biblical-Theological Study of Baptism

This is the one book on baptism that you must read. It was seven years in the making. Doug believes that until a new approach is taken, separations over the meaning, mode, and recipients of baptism will never be bridged.

This new approach traces the roots of baptism deep into the OT Scriptures. When understood properly, we discover that baptism is always the sign that God has used to initiate his people into a new creation. Baptism in the NT is not "new." Rather, it derives its origin from OT predecessors. It has a direct, sacramental counterpart, and it isn't circumcision. It is baptism. When we understand that baptism comes from baptism, especially in its sacramental expression in the priestly covenant, reasons for the NT practice begin to make perfect sense.

Now Baptists have an argument that infant Baptists can finally understand, because we are beginning our argument in the same place. This is an Old Testament covenantal approach to the Baptist position with baptistic conclusions as to the mode and recipients of baptism. That's what happens when we root baptism in baptism rather than circumcision.

Chapters:
The Baptism of Jesus
Baptism and the Sanctuary
Baptism and the Priesthood
Baptism and the Covenant
Implications for Christian Baptism

Available in Paperback or Kindle at Amazon.com

Covenant Theology:
A Reformed Baptist Primer

Covenant theology is often said to be the domain of infant Baptists alone. But there really are such things as Reformed Baptists who believe in covenant theology as a basic system for approaching Scripture.

This primer sets out to give the basics of a Reformed Baptist covenant theology and to do so in a way that is understandable to the uninitiated. It was originally a series we did on Sunday nights at our church. It agrees with classical formulations of covenant theology in that there is a Covenant of Redemption, a Covenant of Works, and a Covenant of Grace in the Bible.

The book takes a multi-perspective approach to the Covenant of Redemption in that this covenant is the basis for the classic formula that Christ's death is sufficient for all, but efficient for the elect. It sees the Covenant of Works for Adam in a broader context of a covenant made with all of creation, a covenant where laws establish the parameters for creation's existence.

It differs from Paedobaptist covenant theology in that it sees the Covenant of Grace as only properly coming through Jesus Christ. OT gracious covenants are typological of the Covenant of Grace but save people on the basis of the coming work of Christ through faith alone. This is the traditional way Reformed Baptists have articulated the Covenant of Grace.

Finally, it sees an entire covenant in the Old Testament as often (but not always) missing from formulations of covenant theology. In the opinion of the author, this "priestly covenant" is vital to a proper understanding of 1. The continuity of the practice of baptism from OT to NT, 2. The answer to why we never find infants being baptized in the NT, and 3. A more precise way to parse the legal aspects of the OT economy, thereby helping us understand why the moral law continues today. This volume works from the basic presupposition that continuity in God's word is more basic than discontinuity. In this, it differs from dispensationalism and new covenant theology. The book suggests that this is the greatest strength of covenant theology, which does also recognize discontinuity.

Available in Paperback or Kindle at Amazon.com

Galatians:
A Supernatural Justification

A play on words, the subtitle of this book gives you the two main points it tries to get across. Galatians central message teaches how a person is *justified* before a holy God. This once precious and central teaching of Protestant theology is often misunderstood or relegated the pile of irrelevant, stale doctrine.

Perhaps that is why the Apostle Paul supercharges his teaching with an oft-overlooked side of this letter - the *supernatural* beings who tempt us and teach us to give up the only truth that will save us. Galatian Christians would have been familiar with these supernatural beings; their culture was steeped in it. Thus, they mistake Paul for the messenger-healer god Hermes, and Barnabas for Zeus. Paul's warning: "Even if we or an angel from heaven should preach to you a gospel contrary to the one we preached to you, let him be accursed." This is Paul's fatherly way of showing his children in the faith that the gospel is paramount; it alone is able to save. Such a warning like this can have new power, as people are returning with reckless abandon to the worship of the old gods.

This book is from a series of sermons preached at the Reformed Baptist Church of Northern Colorado in 2011.

Available in Paperback or Kindle at Amazon.com

The Five Solas
of the Reformation

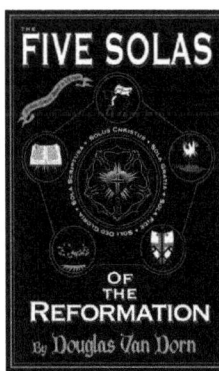

The 500th anniversary of the Reformation occurred in 2017. It was October 31, 1517 that Martin Luther nailed his 95 Thesis to the door of the great cathedral at Wittenberg, Germany. He had no idea what that simple act would do. His bold proclamation and challenge to for Rome to reform her ways and beliefs was met with hostility from some and great sympathy from others. Out of this sympathy arose Protestantism, a movement deeply concerned with grounding all things on Holy Scripture, giving glory to God alone, and recovering for that generation the biblical gospel of Jesus Christ. In five chapters, Doug Van Dorn takes us back to these ancient catch-phrases that once moved a continent. Scripture Alone, Grace Alone, Faith Alone, Christ Alone, and To God Be the Glory Alone became the rallying cry of all who longed to see men and women, boys and girls saved and set free from sin, death, and the devil. The end of the book contains four helpful Appendices on songs, Church Fathers on the solas, a bibliography for further research, and a letter from Martin Luther.

Available in Paperback or Kindle at Amazon.com

www.ingramcontent.com/pod-product-compliance
Lightning Source LLC
Chambersburg PA
CBHW061640040426
42446CB00010B/1506